DIP YOUR TOE INTO
REAL ESTATE INVESTING

Dip Your Toe
into
Real Estate Investing

MARK A. HAYES

Dip Your Toe into Real Estate Investing
© 2024 by Mark Hayes

Library of Congress Control Number: 2023924089
ISBN: 978-1-954676-80-0 (paperback)   978-1-954676-81-7 (ebook)

Although this publication is designed to provide accurate information about the subject matter, the publisher and the author assume no responsibility for any errors, inaccuracies, omissions, or inconsistencies herein. This publication is intended as a resource, however, it is not intended as a replacement for direct and personalized professional services.

Editors: Christian Pacheco
Cover and Interior Design: Emma Elzinga

Printed in the United States of America
First Edition

3 West Garden Street, Ste. 718
Pensacola, FL 32502
www.indigoriverpublishing.com

Ordering Information:

Quantity sales: Special discounts are available on quantity purchases by corporations, associations, and others. For details, contact the publisher at the address above.

Orders by US trade bookstores and wholesalers: Please contact the publisher at the address above.

With Indigo River Publishing, you can always expect great books, strong voices, and meaningful messages. Most importantly, you'll always find . . . *words worth reading.*

Dedicated to John H. Killian Sr.
June 13, 1941 – April 10, 1998

Contents

Preface

THIS BOOK IS WRITTEN IN memory of my second dad. I never called him that, but what I learned from him as a young kid through my teen years influenced me then, as a young adult, and now as a husband and a father. Dr. John H. Killian, Sr., whom I called Papa Doc, was the father of my friend, Frank.

Frank and I were born four weeks apart and became friends in preschool. We were put in the same kindergarten class. We were inseparable to the detriment of our classmates' learning that the principal told my parents we would not be in the same class again. We both had blond hair, played the same sports, and were close in height, constantly measuring who was taller. Teachers and coaches from elementary through high school got us mixed up and called me Frank and called Frank by my name.

Dr. Killian and his wife, Fran, were childhood sweethearts who both grew up poor in Franklin, North Carolina. Frank told me stories of them wearing potato sacks as babies. Dr. Killian broke the mold of rural, poor living by working hard in school. He attended Davidson College and then Wake Forest University Medical school. He became the first fellowship-trained ophthalmologist in Western North Carolina. He became a leader, helping develop a specialty practice for retinal disease. As a kid, I thought it was cool when I learned he conducted eye surgery on Sugar Ray Leonard.

I spent a lot of time at the Killian household. On the weekends, when the weather was nice, after a long work week at his practice and the hospital, Dr. Killian would be working in his garden. At first, I didn't understand why he chose to do manual labor on his time off, but I realized work was engrained in him and he enjoyed it. He could whistle with the best of them, and he whistled loudly while he planted those flowers and vegetables.

His motto was work before play, and Frank and his older brother, Hume, had a list of chores to do. Since I wanted to play, I pitched in with the chores to get things over with faster. Come to think of it, maybe that is why I was invited over so much!

When I became a teenager, I had various jobs, but if I wanted to earn some extra cash, I would go over to the Killian's house to chop wood. They had a den that was heated by a wood-burning stove, so they always needed firewood. For five dollars an hour, that was hard work.

Frank and I had P.E. in eighth grade together, and one day in the locker room, as we were changing clothes, a heard the sound of a bunch of quarters falling out of Frank's pants pockets. I asked him why he was bringing quarters to buy his lunch. He told me he and Hume were operating the coin laundry business at their dad's apartment complex. Then, in high school, I learned a friend and her mom were renting a home near Dr. Killian's office, and it turned out Dr. Killian owned the home. Little did I know, Dr. Killian was a real estate investor.

In 1981, there was a tax reform that accelerated depreciation of structures. Therefore, high-wage earners like doctors were advised by their accountants to buy real estate to lower their tax liability. Dr. Killian purchased homes, apartment buildings, and commercial properties around his office building.

In high school, we hung out a lot in the Killian's finished basement. They had a TV, stereo system, weights for working out, and a hot tub. There was also a wall of cabinetry full of woven baskets and wooden carved masks. It became a large collection of nice Native American art. I learned Dr. Killian would regularly take a workday to drive the two-hour round trip to do ophthalmology for the Cherokee. If a patient was not covered by insurance and could not pay, he worked pro bono. According to Frank, he bought most of them but did receive many as gifts from patients and their family members. I think he felt he could support the artisans and the market they needed for selling their work to keep the art and tradition from dying. He bought the best stuff.

After graduating high school in 1993, Frank followed in his dad's footsteps and attended Davidson College. I attended Vanderbilt University. In the '90s, before we all had cell phones, we would call each other's home phone when we were back in town. If Dr. Killian answered, he always asked how school was and told me how proud he was of me.

After graduating college, I had a job lined up in Nashville at an engineering firm, but it did not start until July. I went home and lived with my parents for the last few weeks before I started. The last week home, I was broke and I needed a few hundred dollars to live off before I received my first paycheck at my new job. I didn't want to ask my parents for more money, so I asked Frank if he thought his dad could help. He told me I needed to ask him. One night when I was at the Killian's, I got the courage to ask for a loan of $600. Dr. Killian told me to come by his office on my way out of town. I went by his office, we said our goodbyes, and he handed me an envelope with a check. Walking to my car, I opened the envelope. It was for $750.

I started my first "real" job out of college and had been told we got paid every two weeks. What I didn't realize is that, after working two weeks, the check is dispersed the following Friday. I had not factored that extra week into the finances. I had a few one-time expenditures getting settled into a new life as an independent, and I lived very frugally for those few weeks. On that Friday of my first paycheck, I had three dollars to my name. Dr. Killian had provided what I needed.

Over the next few months, when I sent a payment to Dr. Killian to repay the loan, I included a short note. It gave me a chance to tell him about my new life in the real world. I came back to Asheville that summer and Christmas, but Frank was doing a teaching program in Japan, so I didn't see Dr. Killian. The following spring came, and one day in April of 1998 I got a call from a friend. Dr. Killian had died in a car accident at the age of fifty-six. He was driving his usual route from his office to the hospital when another vehicle collided with his.

I took some vacation days and drove to Asheville for the funeral. On the drive, I thought of the Billy Joel song "Only the Good Die Young." My friends and I had to get to the funeral an hour before it started to get a seat. During the service, Frank retold a story about his dad befriending Bobby, an African American who cleaned his office at night. They became friends because Dr. Killian would often work into the night dictating charts. Bobby asked him to be his best man in his wedding, and of course Dr. Killian said yes.

After getting choked up and holding in the tears, I walked out of the church. There was a crowd outside just as big as inside. The Killians had close friends over to their house afterwards to celebrate his life. We told stories both funny and serious that helped us all with the grieving. It was after his death that I learned the impact he had on so many others in the community.

Papa Doc never sat down and taught me about finances or real estate, but he didn't have to. I learned by his example. I didn't go into real estate because of Papa Doc, but it was inevitable.

I think about him almost every day. I see him push that wheelbarrow toward his garden, and I hear his loud whistling. I see him driving his old light blue International Scout. I see him eating popcorn out of that wooden bowl, watching football on that small TV in the kitchen. I see him hitting a bad golf shot and not caring one bit. I see him fly fishing in the river in Idaho. I see his smile.

Papa Doc, this book is dedicated to you. I miss you.

Always seek sound advice and rely upon the expertise of real estate professionals, lawyers, and accountants whenever you engage in real estate activities. Also, seek competent legal advice concerning any purchase of any real estate or real property. I highly recommend a thorough education on real estate markets, issues, and investing for optimal success.

Introduction

REAL ESTATE INVESTING IS ONE of the best ways to make a lot of money and build wealth. The trouble is that most people have no idea where to start.

I didn't either.

When I began learning about real estate investing, an overwhelming number of options pulled me in different directions.

After attending a seminar that spoke about buying and holding rental properties, I'd think, *I want to do that!* Then, an experienced investor would say, "Don't buy rentals. Tenants tear up your home, and all the property managers are terrible. Plus, you will get calls in the middle of the night about clogged toilets!"

After crushing my dreams, people told me I should go for "lease options" instead. They would discuss the advantages of lease options but not the pitfalls. This advice inspired me to buy a course on "lease options." These experts, who were more focused on selling courses on real estate topics and convincing potential students that their approach to business was the right one, sent me on a crazy back and forth that continued as I struggled to learn about different aspects of investing. Each time I got excited about new material, I would soon find myself disappointed and having second thoughts.

However, we all have different interests and different strengths and weaknesses. Entering the real estate industry can take a long time for some people. Risk-averse people spend so much time educating themselves that they eventually give up and never invest. Risk takers jump in too quickly and are prone to make costly mistakes. I wrote this book to give you a brief overview of the different types of investing available and then provide steps for entering this trade at a threshold that meets your own capacity for risk.

Since getting my feet wet, I have been involved in hundreds of real estate transactions, renovated and built over 100 homes, and loaned more than $10 million to other real estate investors over a three-year period. Over a twenty-year period, I pieced together more than 100 courses and presentations to share insights about success in this field. Hundreds of people have asked me how they could get started in real estate investing, too. The friends, extended family members, friends of friends, and others who pursued me online or at Real Estate Investors of Nashville (REIN) meetings convinced me to write this book and share my experience. I am delighted to share my passion in these pages and hope that it will help your success.

MY BACKGROUND

I've had an entrepreneurial spirit from a young age, maybe because I was forced to embrace one. When I was twelve years old, my parents told me I was not going to get an allowance. My friends' parents handed them money, so I expected the same. My parents' decision allowed me to think outside the box. In the '80s, every twelve-year-old American boy wanted cash for Cokes, candy, and arcade games. So, I started my first business on the school bus in sixth grade, and my mom was my initial investor. Before the advent of Sam's Club and Costco, there was a small wholesale store in my town that sold bulk items to the public. That's where Mom purchased my first box of Blow Pops at my request, launching my first entrepreneurial endeavor. If you have never had one,

Blow Pops are lollipops with candy on the outside—flavors like grape, cherry, and sour apple—with gum in the middle. The cost for a box of 100 broke down to six cents per lollipop. I brought a limited supply to school each day in a brown lunch bag and sold them after school on the bus ride home for twenty-five cents each; I sold out every day. The back of the bus looked like a pre-teen New York Stock Exchange, with kids crowding around me, yelling, and holding up their quarters. I owed my mom six dollars, but I don't think she ever recalled the loan. I purchased my second box with my earnings and continued daily sell-outs. When the school principal found out what I was up to, my candy selling career was over. However, it sparked something inside me, a problem-solving attitude that continued to grow. I realized I could make money on my own, and the process and work was satisfying.

When I needed extra cash in high school, I would chop wood for my friend's dad, whom I called Papa Doc. After college, I started a lawn care business to pay off student loan debt. I read *Rich Dad, Poor Dad* when it was first published, inspiring me to start helping others part-time with financial planning as an independent contractor. Later on, in 2001, a childhood friend loaned me a cassette tape real estate investing course. It set me on a path that changed my life forever.

WHO IS THIS BOOK NOT FOR?

While I do not want to drive anyone away from real estate investing, the timing might not be right for you to get started if you fall into one or more categories below. But that shouldn't stop you from reading this information to expand your knowledge for future use. You can improve your competency in any area below with time and effort.

No Interest

This book is not for someone that does not have an interest in real estate. This sounds obvious, but if you are wanting to impress your parents, a potential date, or just to make money, you will most likely not finish the book or effectively implement any of the strategies.

"Get Rich Quick" Seekers

This book is not a get-rich-quick scheme. Some speakers and courses preach about the ease of making millions in your first year of real estate—if you buy their course. While a few may have done this, most people who take this approach end up having financial difficulties because they grow too fast without proper safeguards or take on too much risk.

Bad Credit, Bad Behavior

This book is not for someone with bad credit. Ask yourself, "Why do I have bad credit?" Are you going into consumer debt spending more than your income? Do you have a monthly spending budget? The bottom line is that you can improve your credit rating when you pay your bills on time and pay down your consumer debt.

Doing so takes discipline. You should have a goal of paying off all debt within a certain period of time, except for debt leveraged by assets such as property mortgages. I recommend reading *Financial Peace* by Dave Ramsey and implementing his plan to improve your credit. If your credit score is damaged due to divorce, lawsuits, or something other than consumer debt, you should speak to a trusted financial advisor and implement a plan to improve your credit score.

One may have financial literacy but lack self-control. Real estate is a large investment and if you do not manage your basic income and expenses it could be a recipe for disaster.

Low Income

This book is not for someone with low income. If you are having trouble paying for basic needs such as food, clothing, housing, and utilities, you need to concentrate on earning more income to take care of yourself and your loved ones; that always comes first. If you are living paycheck to paycheck to survive, you are probably not ready to invest at this time.

WHO IS THIS BOOK FOR?

The Toe Dipper

This book is for someone who might want to "dip their toe" into real estate investing but does not know where to start. However, this person has a genuine interest in learning what the business is all about and is not going to enter real estate on a whim.

The Alternative Investor

This book is for those who are considered middle to upper-middle class Americans who want to increase their net worth but do not want to become real estate investors full-time. Rather, they prefer to invest outside of the traditional 401k, IRAs, mutual funds, stocks, and bonds.

The Country Club Member

This book is also for higher wealth individuals who do not want to put time in to becoming an active investor and are in a different field than real estate.

The Agent

This book is for real estate agents that are new or have solely focused on retail real estate.

WHAT THE FUTURE HAS IN STORE

Dip Your Toe into Real Estate Investing will provide all the information you need and the steps you should take to begin your first real estate investment. Together, we will examine the different aspects of real estate investing beneath two main sectors: residential and commercial. This book will also discuss the importance of networking and continual education, who you need on your "team" to succeed, understanding values of real estate, and how to do quick "investment math." After the basics, we will explore a few simple strategies on investing in your first property with key actions to take depending on your situation and interests.

The actual purchase is a giant leap, but you will be able to shake any fears or anxiety by discovering teaching systems needed to secure your real estate investment. Following these strategies will help you earn additional income and assets that will change your future, as it did mine. However my journey was not an easy one. I will share with you personal stories of failure and success as lessons learned. Some are funny, some are hard to believe, but I think you will find something to relate to as you begin your real estate journey.

Giving Back

I am donating fifty percent of the net profit from this book to Habitat for Humanity. Habitat for Humanity is important to me for several reasons. Their vision is for a world where everyone has a decent place to live, and their mission seeks to put God's love into action. Habitat for Humanity brings people together to build homes, communities, and hope by providing affordable housing.

Homeowners provide sweat equity in several ways. They work alongside volunteers to help build their home. They may also work at a local Habitat Restore or the local Habitat office. Most importantly, they attend financial education and budgeting planning classes.

I hope this book will help Habitat's vision and mission, and I highly recommend volunteering on a Habitat home build. It is fun, and you will learn some great home maintenance skills.

Chapter 1

The Deep Sea of Real Estate Investing

A GREAT ASPECT OF REAL estate investing is there are so many avenues in which you can invest. However, they can overwhelm a beginner. Ask yourself these questions to help narrow your focus:

- What are your goals?
- What part of real estate investing interests you?
- Does your personality or background favor a type of real estate? For example: construction management, financing, acquisitions
- Are you looking for cash flow, appreciation, a quick small profit, or a large profit in several months?
- What is your financial situation?

There are a lot of options and a lot to learn. I recommend getting to know all you can about one or two types of real estate investing before diving in based on your experience and interests.

The two main categories of real estate are residential and commercial. Simply put, residential real estate provides living space while commercial real estate is used exclusively for business purposes. Different types of properties fall under each of these two categories, and some of them overlap.

TYPES OF RESIDENTIAL PROPERTIES

Most beginner investors start in residential real estate due to the lower risk and cost of entry. There are plenty of options to choose from.

Vacant Land

Vacant land or undeveloped land is usually over five acres. Larger sections of land are referred to as tracts. Some people call tracts *raw land*, meaning they lack public utilities and buildings. Raw land is either open field, wooded, or a combination of both. Fields are mainly flat or rolling topography. Wooded land can vary from flat to hilly to steep. Large tracts are mostly in rural locations.

Zoning uses and density allowed for large tracts are mostly unrestricted and agricultural. Depending on your area's zoning laws, which vary by state and county, raw land can be subdivided into smaller parcels. Uses include traditional sharecrop farming, raising livestock, tree farming, gardening, raising bees, and recreation such as hunting, hiking, and storage.

Determining the value of large undeveloped land can be difficult because the lack of similar properties recently sold in the rural communities. Also, it is rare that two parcels are identical, even perfectly similar. Some factors affecting land value include location, size, topography, allowed uses, installed or accessible utilities, subsurface soils for water wells and septic tank availability, road frontage, fencing, and water features (creeks, streams, ponds, or small lakes).

Vacant Lots

Residential vacant lots are considered smaller properties that are typically five acres or less, with the majority under one acre. A vacant lot's topography, like raw land, can vary and consist of open field or woodlands. Vacant lots are mostly found within neighborhood subdivisions in urban and suburban regions.

Local counties and cities have their own residential zoning codes and regulations governing the use of vacant lots. Construction of a single-family home may be allowed, and, in some cases, a small multi-family building may be as well. Asking your local officials about zoning and codes is essential. Make every effort to get any verbal communication in writing as well. When you choose a lot to evaluate, consider size, the existing zoning and allowable density, topography, utility availability, flood zones, and neighboring lots and homes before making important decisions.

Single-Family Properties

Single-family homes are simply one home for one family unit on one individual property. They range from tiny homes, condominiums, townhomes, houses to larger estates. Condominiums are a building or a complex consisting of individually owned apartment style homes. Townhomes, also referred to as row homes, are usually two or three stories attached with a shared wall.

The property can vary from a very small lot to a large tract of land. Single-family homes are in urban, suburban, and rural communities but typically not in a downtown or central business district, where higher density and commercial zoning is the norm (with the exception of condominiums). Property values depend on the size of the home, the style and design of the exterior and interior, the number of bedrooms and bathrooms, the yard, and amenities such as fireplaces, pools, and garages.

Location is probably the top factor for homeowners given the importance of proximity to workplaces, shopping and restaurants, schools, and the surrounding community.

Multi-Family Properties

Multi-family properties fall under residential and commercial. Residential multi-family homes are typically defined as two to four units on one property. Two connected homes on a property are called a duplex, a three-home dwelling is a triplex, and a four-unit structure is called a quadraplex.

Multi-family properties are mostly in urban and suburban parts of towns and cities, with some in rural areas. Multi-family properties are put into classes labeled A, B, C, and D. Class A properties are new or newer in a prime location, down to D being old, maybe in disrepair, and in less desirable areas. Property values depend on several factors. Once you determine the property class, calculate the number of units, the unit mix (the number of bedrooms and baths per unit), the gross rental income, the average vacancy rate, and all expenses (e.g., property management, taxes, and insurance). You can then determine a rate of return (also referred to as a cap rate).

TYPES OF COMMERCIAL PROPERTIES

Investing in commercial property can be lucrative. In dealing with more complex endeavours and larger capital than residential, collaborations and partnerships are more prevalent for success.

Multi-Family Commercial Properties

Usually defined as five or more units, multi-family commercial properties have different styles such as garden-style low rise apartments, multi-story apartment buildings, and high-rise apartments. Small multi-family properties are units of five up to approximately twenty units. These can be managed by the owner with or without assistance from a resident of the complex or a property manager. Institutions and REITs (a fund consisting of real estate holdings) are not buyers of small complexes, so these are good opportunities for individuals or small partnerships.

A professional property management company with dedicated staff is necessary for the large complexes. As explained in the residential section, multi-family properties can be graded as A, B, C, or D properties based on location, condition, and market rent. Some affordable housing initiatives can be beneficial to both the investor and the community, and there can be certain tax advantages and incentives while the community meets a housing need where tenants are getting priced out of the area. Property values are based on the financials more than residential comparables. The value can be improved by renovations and increasing rents as well as adding amenities for the tenants such as an exercise facility, a swimming pool, picnic areas, and walking trails.

You can gauge the price of a complex on dollars per unit before exploring the deal further. If another multi-family property is selling on average for $80,000/unit and another for sale is listed at $120,000/unit with similar rents, that is a quick indication it is overpriced. A simple method to determine a baseline value is to calculate the capitalization (cap) rate.

The cap rate is the rate of return on the investment, and you need the gross rents and expenses from the past year to calculate that. A general conservative rule if you do not have accurate expenses is 50% of gross revenue. Gross rents minus the expenses (not including loan costs) equals Net Operating Income (NOI). The figure below shows the formula. If a ten-unit complex is for sale for $1,000,000 and the NOI is $70,000 then the cap rate is 7%. There are other factors to consider that experience and advice from experts will share if you dive deeper

$$\text{Cap Rate} = \frac{NOI}{Value}$$

Office Properties

Commercial property for office use can be office complexes for one tenant or multi-tenants and come in all sizes from one-story structures to skyscrapers. The lease holders are businesses, and the terms are typically multi-year with built-in rent increases. Office property value is calculated based on the cap rate and the market of what other similar office buildings have sold for recently.

Retail Properties

Retail property can be small (usually one building with one tenant like a bank or restaurant) or large (including big box stores, strip centers, and multi-tenant buildings). A unique trait of retail development is that some businesses desire to own their building while some prefer to lease the space. Outparcels can also be sold separately to a business or an investor. This is beneficial for the developer because, when selling portions of the project, they lower their costs basis while retaining the remainder of the property for cash flow and appreciation.

Businesses that lease their space will often have a triple-net lease, an arrangement where the tenant pays rent, property taxes, insurance, and maintenance. The term of the lease is long-term, usually with built-in increased rent. A triple-net lease is beneficial to an investor because the income is predictable since the tenant is responsible for expenses. Therefore, a cap rate is easily computed.

Industrial Properties

Industrial properties are suitable for warehouse space, manufacturing, production, assembly, research, storage, date centers, flex space, and distribution. The industrial sector does not seem as popular as an investment compared to other commercial types; however, the businesses within this space are an important part of our everyday life making this sector sustainable now and into the future.

Just look in your house, at your office, and any business you visit to see that the products and materials were once in a warehouse. Industrial properties are often grouped together in sections of a city or county. Since logistics with transportation is important, they are located near interstates and airports, even train railways. There is a mix of business people who prefer to own their building versus lease their space. Triple-net leases are also common for industrial investments. Property values are also determined based on a cap rate.

Hotels/Hospitality

Hotel properties are self-explanatory. There are full-service hotels, limited-service that are smaller (sometimes called boutique hotels), and extended-stay hotels. Hospitality properties aside from hotels can be convention centers and venues for social events such as weddings and concerts.

Mixed-Use Properties

Mixed-use properties are a combination of two or more of the different types of properties. An example seen in cities are retail spaces or restaurants on the first floor with offices or residential above. The live/work concept with a business and residence combined falls under this category.

Vacant Land and Lots

We have previously explored vacant land/lots in the Residential Properties section. The difference here is that commercial land and lots have zoning and land-use types used for commercial purposes. Commercial land refers to areas that are designated for business and drive the economy. The specific land uses for commercial land can vary based on local zoning regulations, urban planning policies, and the needs of the community.

Special Purpose Commercial Property

Special purpose commercial properties that do not fall under the other aforementioned types of properties can be considered miscellaneous properties. These include theaters, zoos, amusement parks, sports/recreation centers, and parking lots. Values of these properties are based on the cap rate as well as the size of the land, structures, and equipment on-site.

No matter what type of real estate investing you prefer, keep these things in mind when evaluating property.

EVALUATING PROPERTY

Before investing in any real estate, there are many elements and features to consider to determine what property is really worth. Keep all of these in mind before purchasing a property.

Location

I am sure you have heard the saying, "Location, location, location." This is the most important aspect of a real estate decision and factors in such things as good schools, traffic, restaurants, and entertainment venues; also consider surroundings such as train tracks, flood plains, and landfills that may impact property values. Properties in desirable locations are relatively expensive, so finding a good deal in a popular location can be difficult. Geographic farming where a real estate agent markets to certain neighborhoods to be successful is a great strategy for an investor. Farming an area and getting to know the people and places very well are imperative in finding deals that can be more affordable and more attractive in the future.

The Numbers

With investing, you have to run the numbers and have the discipline to not go against your calculations. Otherwise, you will not meet your goals. For example, if you want a 10% annual return, do not buy a property that has a 9% return on paper just to get the deal. Move on and find something else. If you have the discipline to move on, sometimes the seller comes back later and takes your offer. You must keep emotion out of your decisions. For instance, remember that homes you're looking to work with will not be your personal residence although, if you make some poor decisions, you might end up living there!

Maintenance/Management

Maintenance and management take time and money. Properties with lower maintenance might cost more upfront but will free up your time and resources to find other deals. The potential return on your investment should be higher with sound maintenance and management practices.

Appreciation

Appreciation is determined when you purchase and when you sell. When you buy, you can affect the appreciation by making improvements. The value is affected by time and the market conditions at the time you sell; is it considered a buyer's market or a seller's market?

Appreciation is also affected by location, as we've discussed earlier. Find out the current zoning, what that allows, and if there is any potential for changes from local officials before making a purchase. Contact the area's neighborhood council representative and other local investors and get their feedback for growth and new developments.

Appeal to the Masses

You need to play the percentages to better succeed in real estate. In a residential neighborhood, would it make sense to buy a two-bedroom, one-bath home if you planned to rehab and sell it when other homes that have sold the quickest for the highest price have three bedrooms and two baths? A general rule is not to own the largest home in a neighborhood.

When working with interior designs, look and see what others are doing and what is popular with your target buyers. If you are leasing a commercial retail space, lease to a business that will appeal to a large population so they can succeed and pay the rent. With multi-family properties, evaluate the unit mix of the property. Unit mix is simply the different number of bedroom apartments in a property and can range from an efficiency up to four bedrooms. A twenty-unit complex with all one-bedrooms will limit your pool of buyers when you sell. A twenty-unit complex with fifteen two-bedroom units and only five one-bedroom units is more marketable.

I learned this lesson the hard way with a home I built to sell a few years ago. My general contractor and I had this idea to put the kitchen and living room on the second floor like some loft style homes in more metropolitan cities. That home sat on the market, and I dropped the price, barely making a profit. Meanwhile, the home we built next door with the living space on the first floor and bedrooms upstairs sold before it was finished, and I made an expected profit. Doing this may not be exciting, but it will be more successful.

There are a lot of choices and decisions that must be made as a real estate investor. Do not be afraid of exploring other avenues once you have some experience. Keep these basics in mind to succeed in any type of real estate.

Chapter 2

Navigating Your Ship

NAVIGATING ANY SEA CAN BE challenging. There are only a few signs and markers. As the captain, you need to know the direction you are going. You must have a strategy and plan to get back to shore.

Now that you are starting to understand how to identify the types of residential and commercial real estate, here are the main strategies for investing in properties.

WHOLESALING

Wholesaling is basically finding a deal, getting the property under contract to purchase, and assigning the contract to another investor and earning a nominal fee. This is a good strategy for beginners because you don't need funds or credit. If you like marketing and are a people person, wholesaling might be a good method to enter real estate investing. You will want to master other skills such as understanding values and construction costs, contract paperwork, and contact management.

Wholesaling can be a strategy for any of the previously discussed properties. However, this method can be time consuming where the reward is earning a small compensation per transaction; with experience, bigger deals can have a large five-figure, even a six-figure fee. Wholesaling is similar to a real estate agent making a commission when acting as a listing agent for the seller. The difference is the agent's commission is paid out by the seller based on a percentage of the sales price. With wholesaling the end buyer pays the assignment fee to the wholesaler. Also, you do not have to be a licensed real estate agent as a wholesaler.

Some not educated in real estate investing have said that wholesaling is illegal, and it can incur fines- and more severe penalties if not done properly. The key is to have proper paperwork and be open and honest to all parties involved. If you are dishonest, sellers will then not trust you and the deal could fall apart. You then do not get paid and your end buyer investor will not want to work with you again.

If I was wholesaling a property, I would say something like this: "Mr. Seller, I work with other investors and partners that are busy rehabbing homes, so they rely on me to find them their next property. I will facilitate this transaction to make it easy for you if you agree to the terms and are okay with me making a fee as long as you don't pay for that, correct?"

"Yes, great," they say.

"I will walk you through the process, and, at the closing, you will get a big check and one of my investors will pay me a fee. Sound good?"

You must use a *contract to purchase* that has an assignment clause per state laws for where the property is located. When the document is signed and legally executed by both parties, you have control of that contract. You must also use a well-executed assignment of contract document once you find an interested end buyer. You then want to use an investor-friendly real estate attorney or title company that also understands these types of transactions.

Believe it or not, some of these professionals are not familiar with wholesaling. Some wholesalers can get in trouble when they market a property before they have it under contract. That is illegal because then they do not control the contract. Therefore, they are acting as a real estate agent. If you do not have a license in that state as a real estate agent and do not have a property executed agreement with that seller, you can get reported to the state's real estate commission.

The steps of wholesaling are as follows:

1. Develop a marketing plan for leads: what price point, areas/ neighborhoods, type of sellers (e.g., out of state owners, owned certain # of years, no mortgage).
2. Purchase a list of leads and send letters and/or postcards or contact via phone.
3. Develop a buyers list: networking, social media.
4. Screen leads and meet with potential sellers.
5. Negotiate a sales contract with seller.
6. Market property to your buyers list.
7. Secure buyer.
8. Facilitate transaction and collect funds after closing.

Here is how a wholesaling transaction may play out. You send letters to potential sellers and receive calls from some interested in selling. You set up appointments to meet the sellers and view the properties. One property needs about $30,000 in renovations. Based on comparables, the home would be worth $270,000 after repairs. You make an offer of $150,000 and the seller agrees.

After the assignable contract is executed, you send the deal to your buyers list for $160,000. A few buyers are interested and you set up a walkthrough with the seller. One of the investors agrees to $160,000. You execute an assignment contract and collect earnest money. You turn in all the paperwork to a title company or real estate attorney.

On closing day, the seller receives $150,000 minus any seller closing costs negotiated and any property tax prorations if owed. You receive $10,000. The end buyer now owns the property.

FLIPPING HOMES

Flipping homes, also referred to as *fix up and sell* or simply *rehabbing,* involves purchasing a property (typically a single-family home), renovating the home, and selling the property to a homeowner. This strategy can also be used with multi-family properties and land as well. The key is making improvements to the property to add value to the next owner.

If you enjoy construction or interior design, rehabbing might be the place for you. Other skills needed to succeed are management, organization skills, and financial skills such as budgeting, bookkeeping, and cash flow management. This investing method can be very profitable but can also encounter numerous risks and pitfalls.

You have probably watched a reality show about flipping homes. Some shows portray flipping homes as an easy, quick, and largely profitable endeavor. However, they don't tell the whole story. Flipping homes has numerous challenges like managing contractors and supplies, selecting design finishes, making numerous decisions, and taking on large liability.

Rehabbing property is time consuming, and I do not recommend getting too involved in manual construction when you have to hire general contractors (and subcontractors) to manage the project. The time from when you purchase, renovate, list to sell, then close to sell can be from a few months to one year or more depending on the size of the project, how the rehab is managed, and how the transaction to sell proceeds.

Most investors' goal are to net twenty percent of the sale price as profit. In addition to costs of renovations, inexperienced investors can fall into the traps of overpaying for the property, underestimating the construction costs, and not factoring in holding costs such as loan fees and interest, taxes and insurance, utilities, and closing costs and commissions to sell the property. Flipping is also taxed as ordinary income and therefore taxed at a high percentage as compared to some long-term investing. A flip that could earn you $40,000 in four months could turn into $10,000 or less after one year if you are not diligent.

Rehab properties can be found from wholesalers, real estate agents, direct marketing, or even *driving for dollars*. Driving for dollars is when you farm an area or neighborhood where you want to invest. If you notice a home with deferred maintenance, it looks vacant, or the yard is not maintained, you ask the neighbors about it or send the property owner a letter stating you want to purchase the property. A low-cost and low-risk of entry into this space is to partner with an experienced "flipper" and exchange your time for their expertise. You can also participate financially as a silent partner and gain education from the active investor.

Follow these steps if you want to explore flipping properties:

1. Secure funding source: your cash, a line of credit, bank loan, hard-money loan, or partner.
2. Develop a budget and scope for the property.
3. Make an offer and purchase the property.
4. Renovate property.
5. Sell with a real estate agent or by owner.
6. Negotiate contract to sell.
7. Go into escrow.
8. Attend the Closing.

This fix and sell is not an actual project but has situations I personally have run into in the past to make it a more realistic scenario. You receive an email from a wholesaler about a deal in a neighborhood you like to invest. After reviewing the photos, price, and closing date, you contact the wholesaler to view the property in person. After due diligence, you and your real estate agent find comparables (comps) of similar sold homes in the area and determine the sales price after renovations would be $260,000. However, factoring in negotiation and possibly the market softening in the next several months your ARV (after repaired value) is $250,000. Your conservative estimate of renovations is $40,000 after consulting with the general contractor you plan to hire. Knowing these two metrics you calculate your maximum purchase price as shown on the next page:

After Repaired Value (ARV)	$250,000
70% of ARV (20% Profit, 10% Holding Costs)	$175,000
Construction Costs (Includes 10% Overages)	$40,000
Maximum Allowable Offer (MAO)	$135,000

The wholesaler had the property listed at $140,000 but agrees to your $135,000 offer. You secure a hard-money loan from a local lender and close the transaction three weeks later. Your contractor begins the project and progresses quickly. About halfway through the project, he tells you they are ahead of schedule and plan to finish in three months instead of four.

You have been speaking to the contractor at least three times a week, and you have been stopping by the property multiple times to make sure steps are not missed. As you make the final selections of light fixtures and pick out the kitchen countertops, the contractor goes MIA. The work comes to a halt for two weeks, and it has been three months, the anticipated completion date.

The contractor finally calls you and tells you he was in a motorcycle accident and is in the hospital. He lost his phone with all his contacts and didn't have your number. He is now recovering at home and plans to be back working in a couple of weeks to come finish your project. Around the four-month mark, subcontractors start showing up again, and one month later the construction is complete, and the home is ready to be listed.

The real estate agent highly recommends staging the home with furniture so that takes an additional week and cost $3,000 of unexpected cost. The agent prices the home at $249,900 but, with the great staging and nice photos online, you get two offers quickly. One offer is $245,000 cash with no loan contingency. The other offer is full price with a loan contingency and closing in forty-five days.

After consulting with your agent, you decide to take the full price offer since the agent spoke to the lender and they assured them they were great borrowers.

The "buyers" hire a home inspector who comes to the property the following week. The inspector notices in the crawl space two floor joists that are cracked. He puts in his report that he recommends the buyers consult a structural engineer. This scares these first-time homebuyers, and they back out of the transaction since they had a home inspection contingency. Your agent then goes back to the buyer who offered cash, but they have already found a different home.

Your agent puts the home back on the market while you hire a carpenter to "sister-on" two new floor joists and pay an engineer for a letter in case the issue arises again with a new buyer.

Within a couple of days you have another full-price offer that you accept. After the new buyers' home inspection, you are asked to fix a small punch list of items. You have already paid your general contractor in full, and so he has no motivation to come back and perform a half day's work for no pay. You cannot reach him, so you hire a handyman to complete the punch list.

The appraiser for the bank does their walk-through of the property one week before the closing date and assures your agent that he will turn in his report to the bank the following day. However, the bank does not receive the appraisal until one day before the closing, and they need at least forty-eight hours to review due to their large volume of loans at the end of the month.

The buyer's agent asks for a one-week extension to close. At this point, your hands are tied, and, if you say no, you will have to attract a new buyer and it could be another forty-five days to close. You agree to the one-week extension. You attend the closing to sign papers one week later on a Friday afternoon, expecting to receive your large cashier's check. However, since the buyer signed at a different title company, the signed documents are not verified before the wire cutoff and the bank does not fund the loan until Monday.

You make a special trip back to the title company on Monday afternoon to receive your funds.

The time of ownership ended up being about eight months. After delays of construction, additional costs, and sale taking longer, your net profit is $30,000 before taxes instead of the $50,000 you expected. After taxes, your net-net profit is approximately $20,000.

If you do several flips over time, some will be very profitable, some will have an expected return, and some will be deemed not worth it. Therefore, to succeed this strategy is best fit for someone who consistently flips versus someone who intends to rehab and sell on occasion or combine this strategy with another to offset the risk.

BUY AND HOLD VACANT LOTS OR RAW LAND

This strategy is what it sounds like. You purchase a vacant lot or land and own it for a time period until you want to sell it to make a certain profit. Buying vacant lots and land is a strategy not many investors gravitate to because of financing issues and low- or no-income production from the property. However, there are many people who have become wealthy from this strategy. If you have some cash or a partner with funding and are looking for a long-term investment and have patience, this might be a good strategy for you. Banks either want a large down payment (25-50%) for land or lots, or they will not finance them unless you can prove income from the property or hold cash reserves. Residential vacant lots rarely produce income unless you are very creative and get support from the community.

You can produce income from larger tracts by leasing them for farming crops, trees, flowers, or other natural resources, livestock, hosting bees, hunting, and storage. Harvesting timber either with a select cut or a clear cut can be a source of income as well; consult a forester prior before purchasing a property with a dense amount of mature timber. There are also government grants available for property land management, and you can save on property taxes by applying for the greenbelt application through your county. This is the Agricultural, Forest, and Open Space Land Act of 1976 which allows certain land to be taxed not on the land's market value but on its present value. Another advantage comes when profits are taxed as long-term gain when you hold the property over one year, a lower tax than from flipping and wholesaling.

Finding deals on lots and land is not difficult. Land and lots often get inherited because it is a long-term hold and the current owner might have no use for the property. Heirs often need cash and want to cash out. They also might not pay the property taxes. Every state county holds tax sales, and vacant land are often on the list. A direct marketing campaign to out of state land owners will generate leads. I have spoken to several property owners over the years that have land in Tennessee but live out of state because they had intentions to move here but, after several years, their life has not changed. For targeting vacant lots, look at emerging neighborhoods where new construction of homes has begun. You can research the cost of what builders have paid for lots with assistance from your real estate agent or looking at tax records online.

Follow these steps if you invest in vacant properties:

1. Secure funding source: your cash, a line of credit, bank loan, hard-money loan, or partner.

2. Choose an area where you desire to own land. For example, in the U.S. begin with a state, then a region, then narrow down by county.

3. Narrow down the type and size of land. Your purchase price range will be a factor. For example, urban, suburban, or rural. Lots under one acre, one to five acres, five to twenty acres, twenty-one to fifty acres, fifty-one to one hundred acres, one hundred-plus acres.

4. Generate leads. Launch direct marketing campaign by sending letters and/or postcards to property owners. Contact real estate agents who specialize in land for that area. Search Land.com and other land for sale websites.

5. Interview property owner about the property. Ask if they have a survey. Ask about the utilities, zoning, the topography, percent wooded versus field, if fencing is installed, and if there are any water features.

6. Visit the property, if possible, and research other nearby properties to determine value.

7. Make an offer, negotiate if needed, and get property under contract if you decide to pursue.

8. Purchase the property.

9. Apply for the greenbelt and explore any income producing methods if you desire.

10. List the property to sell once values have gone up.

In 2015, I had been building new spec homes for over three years and the boom of new construction in the urban neighborhoods of Nashville was in full force. Lot values were pushing up higher, but I was still able to find some great deals, so my income was going to be higher than the previous years and I needed a place to invest other than in urban development

I have been blessed with a beautiful family, and my three boys and girl were between the ages of two and seven. We were finally almost out of the diaper stage. My wife and I were seeing our kids' generation already addicted to television and video games. We desired some land where they could explore nature, go on hikes, camp, and fish. Maybe we would eventually build a home farther out of Nashville and retire there.

We zoned in on Hickman County west of Nashville due to the proximity of our current residence. Hickman County also has some affordable beautiful land (back in 2015) and a low population. Since I was a real estate agent, I set up a MLS search for myself so new listings would be emailed to me daily. About once a month, I would go look at property, learning more about the area each time. I remember my GPS at the time taking me down small dirt roads with a creek crossing over it that was undriveable even in my old Land Cruiser. Some properties I couldn't find based on the listing agent's directions, or my GPS and my cell phone would not get a signal so I couldn't call the agent. I saw some properties that were nice and a lot I did not desire.

I came to realize that, if the property was forty-five minutes to an hour from our house, we would probably not go there as often. I narrowed down my search to East Hickman County. After almost a year, I came across a listing, and the first photo was this beautiful mini waterfall from a creek. It was fifty-five acres for $189,900. Once I did a little more research and saw it was thirty-five minutes from our home, I got excited and made plans to drive out there the next day. If you have purchased your home, you probably had a feeling when you pulled into the driveway or entered the home that "this is the one."

As I drove closer to this property, I saw some beautiful farmland with nice horse fencing and some higher-end homes. I started to get that feeling, "this could be the one." I saw the For Sale sign and started walking the property. The front portion was open rolling field. I was intrigued, but I was looking for the beautiful creek. I walked into the woods and saw a dry creek surrounded by amazing large mature trees. I called my wife and said, "I think I found the property we have been looking for, when can you come out here?" I called the listing agent, and he informed me the creek was in the back of the property and that he could meet me there the next day and bring a four-wheeler to explore the property.

The next day, I meet the agent and, after unloading the four-wheeler, we jump on and drive out through the middle of the open field. To the left, alongside some trees, were a few deer, and they hopped into the woods. Now I was really getting excited.

We go to the back of the property to the picturesque creek, and I was sold. This is what we had been looking for, and I was ready to make an offer. The family graveyard with the easement access did not bother me. People can show up anytime to visit family graveyards, and this one was certainly unique; if you could walk through the hills or drive up with a four-wheeler, you'd find the resting place of a Confederate soldier. This was an inherited property, and about six heirs plus their spouses had to sign the contract, but, after about a week, I had it under contract for $187,500, plus I received a buyer's commission of 3%. With funds from selling homes in 2015, we purchased the property in cash.

Since owning the property, we have installed a pond and stocked fish in it, installed a wood horse fence along the road, installed a water well, created driveable paths to access the back of the property, received grant funds from the EQIP program through USDA for land management practices, harvested timber, and have greenbelt status. The property value has increased significantly, and I have a line of credit on the property to have funds available for making other investments.

LAND DEVELOPMENT

Residential land development, also referred to as speculative (spec) building is typically described as vacant parcels where single family homes up to three or four units are constructed. This strategy is similar to flipping homes. The difference is developing new construction from the ground up versus renovating an existing home. The county or municipal zoning will dictate what can and cannot be constructed with any additional restrictions. If a developer has a vision and plan to build a project that is not allowed due to zoning, then they must go through either a board of zoning appeals or through a lengthier process to have the property re-zoned. Each county and municipality have their own process, so navigating this process can be difficult even for the experienced developer. Considerations such as setbacks from the property line, ratio of structure to lot size, height of structure, ratio of pervious to impervious materials for stormwater management, and utilities factor into the site plan, project, and design.

The most important factor besides zoning is utility availability. Finding out the locations of water, sewer, electrical, and natural gas is essential and will determine the value of the land. The expense can be costly and take extra time coordinating with utility companies if the city or county requires you, as the developer, to extend utilities to access the property. More rural areas without municipal sewer will require a septic system. A perk test from a soil scientist will determine the maximum number of bedrooms for the home. This is a geologic exploration that also determines the expense for a septic system installation or even the possibility that a septic system cannot be installed. For instance, the site might be deemed unbuildable if shallow bedrock is located throughout the site.

If city water is not available, you can install a well. Costs can vary depending on the depth of the well needed to attain water. There are also sites where water is not located at reasonable depths or even drinkable; water can also be delivered to homes in remote areas.

In addition to the property itself, a developer needs a team of professionals to improve their investment. Consider hiring a land surveyor (or civil engineer), architect, designer, general contractor (GC), and a great real estate agent.

A land surveyor will determine or validate the property boundaries. They will also develop the site plan based on your home design that will be submitted to attain the building permit. An architect and designer will help with the house plan, overall design of the exterior and interior, and assist in selections for the home. Hiring or partnering with a competent general contractor is also a key component to success. Providing an equity partnership versus a fee structure can incentivize the GC to complete projects speedily and under budget. Building relationships with bankers or financial partners factor into the price range of homes you are building and the volume you can build simultaneously. Partnering with a real estate agent who has a pulse on what buyers are wanting and are great with transactions will help your bottom dollar.

An advantage to new construction over rehabbing a home is that the "hard costs" are easily calculated. Renovating a home can uncover unexpected issues that drive up the costs. New construction costs can be easily calculated upfront. Timing, of course, is of the essence. For example, if lumber costs have a large increase from when the project is estimated till the lumber is ordered, the overage will either eat into the net profit or some design considerations might need to be changed mid project to save on other line items.

Doing upfront due diligence is imperative in your role as developer and to making a profit. Putting yourself in the shoes of the homebuyer and including amenities similar or better to the surrounding homes will determine your success. Managing the finances and general contractor is a large part of the developer's role. Done well, building two to three homes annually can generate a six-figure income.

If you are a beginner real estate investor, you may want to enter the development space as an apprentice. Seek out a local developer who is successful and ask if you can assist them with your time for free in return to learn the business; this might lead to a partnership down the line. You could also ask to work with the general contractor to learn the construction side of the business. If you have adequate funds, you can invest as a silent partner with a developer. If you have funds tied up in a retirement account, you can explore moving them into a self-directed IRA. You could then lend those funds to a developer with a stated rate of return or an equity stake. There are some great tax advantages to this strategy, but confer with an accounting professional before doing so.

The steps of residential land development are as follows:

1. Secure funding source: your cash, a line of credit, bank loan, hard-money loan, or partner.

2. Develop a budget and scope for the property.

3. Make an offer and purchase the property.

4. Pre-Construction phase: Survey, site-plan, demo, tree removal, site prep if necessary.

5. Design and Construction phase: architectural drawings, hire a general contractor, make design decisions.

6. Sell with a real estate agent or by owner.

7. Negotiate contract to sell.

8. Escrow phase: Buyer's home inspections and appraisal

9. Closing: Sign papers and collect funds

LONG-TERM AND SHORT-TERM RENTAL PROPERTY

Owning residential rental property is simply an agreement between the landlord or property manager to a tenant who agrees to pay to reside in the home for a period of time with certain rules and guidelines. Some properties can be purchased with a tenant(s) and a written lease in place, and income is generated at the start of ownership. You may need to perform some minor repairs or improvements up to a major renovation to get a vacant property rent ready.

Like flipping homes, the condition and design of the home will affect the value, thus the rent amount you can achieve. You need to determine if you will manage the property or hire a property manager. Property management involves marketing to attract tenants, leasing the property, collecting rent, and maintenance. Some factors in making this decision are time, cost, and any management experience you may have.

Short-term rentals are somewhat of a newer rental strategy outside of vacation rentals. The boom of this business began with Airbnb, as you may well know. However, this is a much different type of rental and management than long-term rentals. Investigating the city and county regulations for the specific property is imperative, as a permit may be required.

To determine market rents, a *dynamic pricing* analysis should be performed. These can be completed by a short-term rental property manager. Dynamic pricing software calculates the highs and lows of daily rents and vacancies depending on time of year and events in the property area. Short-term rentals require you purchase furniture, artwork, household items, and other amenities to attract guests. Reliable cleaning crews are essential, especially when someone checks out and new guests check in the same day; additional state and local hotel taxes are charged. Occupancy and rent amounts are dependent on reviews of others, so a great guest experience is important. Short-term rentals can result in higher revenue than long-term rentals but, due to being more time-consuming, short-term property managers typically charge double or higher than a traditional property manager for a long-term rental.

Rental property evaluation involves steps similar to flipping homes, in addition to determining the market rent for the property. Much like sales comps, you can also find long term rental comps via Zillow or Rentometer.com. Analyzing net income and cash flow is completed by using the gross rents researched minus all expenses and loan payments, if applicable. Expenses include property management fees, property taxes, insurance, vacancy, and maintenance. Novice investors self-managing the property often do not calculate property management. The investors' time to manage must be considered.

In addition to cash flow, long-term holds have advantages such as value appreciation, lower income tax of passive income, depreciation over time (also a tax advantage), tax-deductible interest, and lowering the principal balance if a loan is on the property.

Purchasing rental property as a strategy to hold over a long period is the best strategy to building wealth in real estate, in my opinion. The irony is that some of my first mentors in real estate spoke against owning rentals. One mentor only told me the horror stories of tenants, collecting rent, evictions, clogged toilets, and getting emergency maintenance calls in the middle of the night. A tenant pouring Quikrete down the toilet or painting the entire apartment black before moving out aren't rejected sitcom premises; they are real situations that can damage your property and pocketbook. The other mentor shared about how all property managers were terrible. He said they were unorganized, not professional, and would steal your money.

If you wish to own a residential property, consider these steps:

1. Secure funding source: your cash, a line of credit, bank loan, hard-money loan, or partner

2. Develop a budget and scope for the property, if needed.

3. Make an offer and purchase the property.

4. Hire contractor for renovations, if needed.

5. Hire a property manager or self-manage.

6. Screen applicants and lease property.

7. Refinance on long-term loan

The advice of those first mentors scared me into other strategies as a novice, with the exception of my first purchase. For the first five years after college, I rented a home with a roommate, a cheap modular home near the Vanderbilt University campus. My roommate and I dubbed it "the double-wide" even though it was not technically a mobile home. I was able to attack my debt by paying less than $500 a month in rent and taking on other side jobs such as mowing grass and working at Tennessee Titans football games (while working full-time).

One of my first mentors, Steve, got a lead on a home in West Nashville that had an "in-law" apartment. He got the property under contract and wanted to wholesale it. I was familiar with the location, but it wasn't like the nicer neighborhoods where my friends were renting or buying. The former owner had some interesting décor choices. One bedroom I called the AC/DC room; it had black textured walls with a bright white popcorn ceiling. I named another bright pink bedroom the Barbie Doll room.

This property was a great opportunity for me to enter the investing world. I had built up my credit score by then and was able to get a FHA loan to structure the deal with Steve; this way, I also had some funds to do some cosmetic work to the home. Steve wanted to help by giving me some of his contractors to do some of the work. I could paint the inside and do some other work since I had the time and needed to save money. I wanted to live in the main part of the home that was larger and nicer and rent out the in-law apartment.

Steve gave me the advice to live in the apartment and rent the larger portion. Since I was single, the rent would cover my expenses of the loan and utilities and allow me to essentially live free. So, I begrudgingly took his advice and purchased my first property in August 2002.

Steve was correct. After about $10,000 in costs plus some of my labor, I had about $90,000 in the property with very little cash spent out of my pocket. I had it appraised within the first year and was able to get a second mortgage line of credit to purchase another property. I lived there for almost three years until I got married. I have since converted the home back to a true single-family home and still own that property twenty years later. Today, it rents for $1570/month and is valued in the $300,000 range as-is. In the past three years, the property has produced a net operating income (NOI) just under $10,000 per year.

Chapter 3

Testing the Waters

I WAS A POOL RAT as a kid. A typical summer day had my mom or dad dropping me off at the tennis courts, and, after an hour or two of playing tennis, I would walk up to the pool, change, and jump right in. It was risky; sometimes it was freezing; other times it felt like bathwater; other times it was just right. Nowadays, I dip my toe in the pool first. I want to know the temperature and feel what I am getting into and assess the situation before taking the plunge. In other words, testing the waters.

This is the same methodology to take into real estate investing. Diving in headfirst is risky. If you jump in unknowingly and it is too cold or too hot, you will jump out and not want to get back in. You can better test the waters by networking with others and furthering your own real estate/ investment education. The amount of information is overwhelming, so learning in the areas that interest you, as well as meeting experienced investors and professionals, will give you the comfort to jump in.

In December 2001, I was visiting my family in Asheville. I stopped by my good friend Zach Young's home on my way out of town. Even though Zach didn't have a full-time job, he was living in the second home he had recently purchased.

"How are you buying these properties?" I asked.

We sat down and, with a legal pad, he wrote out the numbers of a deal. Now I was really intrigued. As I said goodbye to head back to Nashville, he let me borrow the Carlton Sheets course, "No Money Down."

Years ago, if you ever had trouble sleeping and turned on your TV in the middle of the night and started flipping channels, you might have seen Carlton Sheets selling his real estate course. I popped the first cassette into the stereo of my Saturn sedan and listened for the five-hour drive back home. I didn't understand a lot of the terms discussed in the course, so I rewound sections to hear them again, but I quickly moved from intrigue to excitement. I finished listening to the cassettes and read through the booklet when I got home, and over the next few months I then listened to the course a second time and better understood the material. I began practicing what the course taught.

More than one person recommended I join Real Estate Investors of Nashville (REIN), a non-profit focused on education and networking. I looked up advertisements in the classifieds of the newspaper for homes that were sold "As Is" or listed as "Handyman Special."

I called one ad, and the seller was a real estate investor. I started using the script from the Carlton Sheets course to ask him questions.

"You have the Carlton Sheets course, don't you?" he asked. Busted!

I didn't know what I was doing, but I was enjoying chasing deals and talking to other investors that I could learn from. I met an investor through REIN who was selling a home near a local vocational college in East Nashville. He rented out individual rooms to the students who were mostly eighteen to twenty years old. The school was a twelve-to-fifteen-month term, so there was a lot of turnover. I ran the numbers from what the Carlton Sheets course taught me, and it seemed like a cash cow.

The seller showed me the ranch style home, and it was like a fraternity inside. I recall six to eight boys living there with a pool table, posters of scantily clad women on the wall, and beer bottles everywhere. None of that scared me. My lack of experience didn't realize that the price to buy was high because it was based on cash flow and not that it was a single-family home. If the home reverted back to a rental for a single family, it would lose money if I had a mortgage.

The seller was not interested in doing owner financing, but he was confident I could get a loan even though I didn't have any money for a down payment or a full-time job. As he wrote up the contract for me to purchase, I went from excited to nervous. He was asking me questions as he filled in the blanks of the paperwork, and I didn't know the answers. He helped me through the process, but it was later evident that the deal was more in his favor than mine. He referred me to a lender, and, after a couple of phone calls, it was apparent that the home was overpriced and I was not going to be able to get a loan.

Fortunately, that deal did not work out. I would have been managing an illegal multi-family operation of teenage boys across town from my house. It would have been a true "school of hard knocks" for a first investment. As with other investing avenues, if you are not educated and well connected, you can easily make a bad investment like I almost did. Therefore, the two important keys to succeed in purchasing a real estate investment property are education and networking.

NETWORKING

I believe networking leads to proper education. Conversely, education may or may not lead to networking. Interacting with real players in a field will not only teach you and give advice but also refer you to others who can recommend education that helped them. On the other hand, you can read all the books, blogs, and articles about a topic, but if you do not meet others who are in the business, you can get stuck in what some term "analysis paralysis." In other words, networking will give you the confidence to take action.

The first thing to do is to find all real estate investing groups locally and visit them. These groups will help with networking and education. Visit websites like nationalreia.org and look up the nearest local chapter. In most cities, there are some other local clubs or groups that may meet for breakfast, lunch, or dinner. Within these groups, you will meet and find out who the wholesalers are in the area. Get on their lists so they will email or text you when they have a deal.

Seek out the real players and offer to take them to lunch or to shadow them for a day. When I was calling and meeting investors as a newbie, I received two recommendations from more than one person: Join REIN and take Hal Wilson to lunch. When getting the same advice from more than one person, I act and so should you. Hal Wilson was a residential real estate investing legend in Nashville. To give you an idea, here is an excerpt from his obituary when he passed away at the age of sixty-six in 2010 from a long battle with cancer:

"Hal was the industry leader in real estate investment and renovation, with over forty-one years of involvement in just about everything real estate related. His true passion was education in the industry and trained over 50,000 students and individuals. Hal will be remembered as a man with a great attitude, enthusiasm, and lover of negotiation. He was always after the best deal and enjoyed the game tremendously. He was a consummate people collector, and everyone he met became a friend who admired, respected, and genuinely loved him."[1]

When I contacted Mr. Wilson and offered to take him to lunch, he said "Sure!"

At lunch, he told the story about a man who came to his office one day. From this man's appearance, Mr. Wilson thought he was homeless, but Hal greeted him and offered him some coffee. He then found out that the man owned rental properties he wanted to sell. That story was a good reminder to treat everyone with respect.

Hal graciously met with me a couple more times over the next few years and happily gave great advice for my business every time. He is a main reason why I have paid it forward by giving my time to meet with new investors over the years when others have contacted me.

Even if you, like me, don't like social media for personal use, I recommend joining real estate investing Facebook groups for cities you want to invest. With more experience, you will be able to tell the

---

1   "Hal E. Wilson Obituary," *The Tennessean*, April 17, 2010, https://www.legacy. com/us/obituaries/tennessean/name/hal-wilson-obituary?id=23435408.

real players from the others and will be more comfortable in joining other social media platforms such as LinkedIn and Clubhouse; check the Recommended Reading and References at the end of the book for some valuable resources. Some think LinkedIn is just an online résumé site, but it's a powerful business networking site that could generate a deal or connect you to a partner. Hiring a marketing professional who specializes in LinkedIn might be a worthy investment. Clubhouse, on the other hand, is an application where one can find various groups on real estate investing. You join group calls that can be educational may lead to connections to foster possible partnerships or referrals.

Another recommendation is to seek out the right real estate agent, not a friend or family member who has their real estate license on the side or an agent that specializes in retail residential for buyers and sellers. A lot of agents say they will help you even though that is not their niche. You want to seek out a full-time real estate agent who is experienced with investments but is not a full-time investor. Why? Because you want them calling you first when they come across a deal.

EDUCATION

When you make a connection with a real player, ask them what books they read when they got started. Ask them what books they have read or listened to recently; Audible is a great way to listen to books while driving in your car or exercising. Some books I have benefited from are listed at the end of this book in Appendix A. These are not necessarily real estate investing books but books about business, finance, and entrepreneurship. BiggerPockets.com is a great resource with numerous articles, blogs, videos, forums, tools, and even a "find a real estate agent" section. They also hold an annual conference. There are numerous podcasts and YouTube channels on real estate investing. Seek out the ones with great reviews.

Search for seminars and live events that cover real estate investing. Most speakers also sell courses about a topic they specialize in or offer an all-day seminar or multiple-day boot camp. In the early 2000s, if the speaker seemed passionate and genuine, and it was a topic that interested me, I would buy their course. It was usually a large three-ring binder with CDs and a workbook to read. I still have a bookcase of courses in my office. These days, the courses are sold online. Some courses seem expensive to a new investor. However, isn't investing a few thousand dollars into your education to build long term wealth worth it?

Of course, there is usually no better education than the school of hard knocks, otherwise known as on-the-job training. However, you don't have to learn the hard way with your investment or spending your funds. You can shadow another investor to learn their ins and outs of a typical day or week. I shadowed an investor I met early on and ended up buying my first two properties from him.

You can also offer to intern with a full-time investor, exchanging your time for experience and mentorship. My friend Julio Barreto's company, BREADCORP, has a program that provides consultative services to individuals and couples seeking to invest in real estate. He invests in residential homes in the Baltimore, Maryland, area and welcomes partners with no experience to walk alongside the process. The great attribute of his program is that you don't need to live in Baltimore. This is a real example of dipping your toe into real estate investing.

I learned to farm areas early on in my investing career. Not planting seeds and growing crops, but getting to know a zip code or area of town very well. Have you ever driven through a neighborhood and seen the same real estate agent's sign in multiple yards? That real estate agent probably farmed that area to get clients. This is the same for investing.

Early in my career, I chose West Nashville neighborhoods like Sylvan Park, Sylvan Heights, the Nations, and Charlotte Park. West Nashville was close to where I was living near Vanderbilt University, still affordable in the early 2000s, and had potential for further growth. I drove over to Sylvan Park after work and began pounding the pavement. I would get some exercise, and, if people were in their yards, I would stop and ask if they knew any neighbors thinking about selling their property. This is a great way to meet people but also figure out potential sellers and pricing of a market. If you have a dog, take them with you. Most people are more approachable when they can come to you and pet your dog!

There are real estate resources online now like Zillow, Trulia, and Realtor.com. You can research your "farm" and look up what has sold in the past six to twelve months. You can see what homes are listed for sale currently, as well as homes for rent. Ask other investors you meet their opinion on the area. Once you find a real estate agent, ask them to set up a search to send you daily emails for new listings in your area. When you see properties priced lower than the others, it will trigger you to investigate them further.

A common question with new real estate investors is "Should I get my real estate license?" If you are just starting to invest, take some time first to feel out how much you enjoy it. Once you get your feet wet and you want to dive in with intentions of investing on a regular basis, then you should consider the pros and cons of having a real estate license. I wrote a blog for my Website (www.BridgeSouthInvestments.com[2]) in 2021 titled, "Do you have your real estate license?" that may help you make decisions.

We all have busy lives, so carve out just one or two hours a week initially to network and learn; review the action items on education and networking below. Doing a couple of these items will produce the connections and experience to lead you to your first real estate deal. More time and more action might just speed up the time to acquire that first property.

- Locate all local real estate investing groups, visit them, and join the legitimate groups and get involved.

- Seek out experts and take them to lunch or dinner. See how you can offer them value from your background and experiences to them.

2   Mark Hayes, "'Do You Have Your Real Estate License?' — Bridge South Investments." *Bridge South Investments*, February 23, 2021, https://www.bridgesouthinvestments.com/blog/do-you-have-your-realestate-license.

- Join real estate investing Facebook groups for cities you want to invest.

- Find a real estate agent with investing experience.

- Read recommended books.

- Visit real estate investing educational Websites like BiggerPockets.com

- Shadow or participate in a cooperative partnership with a full-time investor.

- Farm an area or areas gathering market research.

Chapter 4

Jump in Feet First

EVERY TIME I HAVE GONE to the beach since I was a kid, the first thing I do is walk down to the edge of the water and stand still. A small ocean wave brings water to first cover my toes, then my feet. The sand turns soft as the water flows from me and my feet slowly sink a little bit into the ground. The feeling is both exhilarating and comfortable as I soak in the sounds of the waves, the breeze, and the feeling of the water and sand. If you are a beachgoer, you have probably experienced this similar feeling.

Once you have the knowledge and connections with real estate investing, it is time to prepare and create a strategy for purchasing your first property. If you are in the corporate or sales worlds, you probably roll your eyes when someone says the term "goal setting." I first heard over twenty years ago that only 3% of people have written goals; you can do an online search for goal setting statistics and find that same stat.

In Stephen Covey's *Seven Habits of Highly Effective People*, he states, "begin with the end in mind." [3] This is just another way to say, "set goals." I admit that I have not written goals consistently, but, when I do, I have looked back at them later and achieved most of those goals.

---

3   Stephen R. Covey, *The Seven Habits of Highly Effective People : Restoring the Character Ethic*, Free Press EBooks, 1989, https://ci.nii.ac.jp/ncid/BA72094375.

Take out a piece of paper, a sticky note, or index card and write "I will purchase my first investment property within X number of months." You decide on the time. Now put that paper where you see it every day like your bedroom or bathroom mirror.

Benjamin Franklin was a versatile man during his lifetime. He was a writer, scientist, inventor, printer, and publisher, to name a few achievements. He was one of the Founding Fathers of the United States, a drafter and signer of the Declaration of Independence, and the first United States Postmaster General. Until I wrote this book, I didn't realize he also coined the phrase, "Time is money."[4]

We all have the same amount of time per day, so delegation is an important key to purchasing your first investment property. I like calling it "spread your web wide." Tell friends and family what you are doing and let them know that, if they send you a deal and you purchase, you will pay them a $1500 referral fee. Post on social media. Inform all real estate agents that you meet what your criteria is to purchase. As suggested in Chapter 2, get on as many wholesalers' buyers lists as possible.

HOW TO THINK LIKE AN APPRAISER

During my first real estate transaction, I received a copy of the appraisal, and I was surprised to see the value of the property as I thought it would be higher. I had found other comps nearby that were not used in the appraisal. Confused and frustrated, I called the appraiser to ask these questions. The appraiser confidently explained why they chose the comps in the report and why they did not use the ones I expected. Each time I spoke to an appraiser, I learned more about their reasoning. Eventually, I better understood values, and doing so helped me tremendously to act fast when a great deal comes across my desk. It even prompted me to write a blog post about thinking like an appraiser

---

4   "Benjamin Franklin," Wikipedia, August 19, 2023, https://en.wikipedia.org/wiki/Benjamin_Franklin.

that appears on my business Website. [5]

In the fall of 2019, I received an email from a wholesaler for two adjacent properties for sale. One was a 4,000 square-foot duplex at the end of a quiet street. The second parcel was a hilly forty-eight-acre property also adjacent to an interstate, with a cell phone tower at the top. The total price was $400,000.

It was a Friday afternoon, and since I immediately knew this could be a great deal, I stopped what I was doing, drove by the properties, and called the wholesaler to ask some questions and set up a time to view the property. I ended up purchasing these properties because I was the first call to the wholesaler. I knew values in that area, so I made it a priority.

A couple of weeks later, I was driving down the interstate with my three boys. I pointed at the cell tower and said, "Boys, you see that hillside, I just purchased that property."

My oldest son asked, "What do you plan to do with it?"

Thinking that was a great question for an eleven-year-old, I replied, "Probably just resell it."

He scoffed.

"Why would you do that?"

I asked, "Have you ever heard of buy low, sell high?"

He paused, then asked, "Is that a crime?"

I had a contractor clean out the duplex, and, based on the funky floor plan and cost to renovate, I chose to resell it "as is." I had a bulldozer operator cut a path through the hillside to create a path to expose the magnificent trees on the property. I hired a forestry specialist who put a bid to harvest a select cut of the mature trees. I then hired a real estate agent to perform an online auction to sell both properties. They both sold in less than five months after purchase, and it was the most profitable deal of my career. It would have been sold to someone else had I waited to call the wholesaler the following Monday.

---

5   "How to Think like an Appraiser — Bridge South Investments," *Bridge South Investments*, April 26, 2021, https://www.bridgesouthinvestments.com/blog/how-to-think-like-an-appraiser.

THE KING'S PAD

If a real estate investor has said they have never lost money on a deal, they are either lying or have not been in the business long enough. Back in 2005, I was running ads in the real estate wanted section of the newspaper; that was a great lead generator back then, believe it or not.

I got a call from a guy, Kenny, who was foreclosing on a home and asked me if I wanted to buy the property.

I responded by asking questions about why he was foreclosing and specifics about the property. His answers piqued my interest in pursuing the investment further.

Then he said, "Now, there is one other thing . . . . There is a guy who lives in the mother-in-law suite in the back, and his name is Elvis Presley Jr.

"Excuse me?" I said quickly.

I viewed the interior of the home except for Elvis Jr.'s apartment. My plan would be to open up the home to a true single family. The basic deal was to purchase the property for $75,000 after Kenny foreclosed on the property. I budgeted $50,000 and expected to sell the property for over $200,000 based on comparables.

Kenny (a private individual) held the mortgage on a property that was bought by a military man and his wife (Sara). Kenny thought that was a safe investment. A few years later, the husband passed away. The wife's doctor (Roger) then allegedly swindled Sara into adding him to the deed of the home in lieu of paying for her medical bills. This doctor also had a patient named Elvis Jr. Elvis later moved into the back of the home.

Sara and Roger co-authored a book called *The Biggest Secret of Elvis' Life Never Before Told*. This short book was about Sara having an affair with the *real* Elvis Presley. Sara passed away after the book was self-published. Roger owned the property with Elvis Jr. living in the back apartment. Roger then got arrested and was sent to federal prison for medical fraud. Due to the doctor's imprisonment, Kenny, the private mortgagee, got the property back by foreclosure.

At the foreclosure sale, several hundred thousand dollars of liens related to the medical fraud were wiped away. Meanwhile, Elvis Jr. was living in the back apartment and had never paid a dime in rent.

This is where I stepped into the deal.

Before I purchased the property, Kenny had warned me that Elvis Jr. had no job, no car, and he watched his big screen TV most of the day. He also warned me that Elvis Jr. decorated his place "a little different." Before too long, I wanted to let Elvis know that a company (my company) was buying the property and that he would have to move soon.

It was the middle of a summer day, and his apartment looked dark. Not knowing what I would encounter, I nervously knocked on the door, took two steps back, and waited. After about fifteen seconds, a head popped up through the light of the door. I thought, *Oh my gosh, he actually has hair like Elvis*. He was wearing an early '70s Elvis style jumpsuit and large gold sunglasses. My heart was pounding.

"I was sent here to—"

Before I could finish my sentence, he said, "Well, Sara left the house to me."

"Okay," I responded.

He invited me to come inside, which I did not want to do. But I had to get my point across that he needed to move.

Words cannot adequately describe what that place looked like (I have photos to prove this). Elvis Jr. informed me he painted all the rooms himself with five coats of textured paint topped with glitter he blew out of his hand onto the surface while the paint was still wet (he demonstrated this method to me. Contractors, take note.) The kitchen was royal blue and gold with music notes pasted on the cabinets. The bathroom was dark red and gold with a matching gold claw foot tub and a toilet seat with the initials *E.P.* His bedroom was purple and black.

For about one and a half hours, Elvis Jr. continued a monologue with stories ranging from how Country Music Television was his idea to how he wanted to partner with the company buying the property by contributing sales proceeds from his CD (he sang for me with Elvis playing in the background).

Again, Elvis Jr. stressed that Sara told him he could have the house before she passed away. Of course, there was no written record proving that claim. Before I left, he gave me a copy of *The Biggest Secret of Elvis' Life Never Before Told*, which included fake photos of Sara posed with her famous supposed lover.

I left and still felt nervous after my encounter with "The King's Son." The last two hours seemed like a wasted afternoon, but at the same time this was a story to tell my future grandchildren.

I purchased the property and started the renovation and the eviction process for Elvis Jr. However, Elvis Jr. was not getting the picture that it was time to go. After the roofers knocked and banged on Elvis Jr.'s roof, and after his electricity was cut off when his relative refused to pay his bills, he started to open up to the idea of moving.

Eviction court day came, and I thought, *This guy doesn't have a car, nor a leg to stand on for this case, so he won't show.* The court clerk started roll call. I kept looking around, but there was no Elvis in sight. Finally, he sneaked in the back. My heart started pounding. What made him decide to come?

After the roll call and before the case began, I pulled Elvis aside and found out his intentions. He was there to state his case to the judge that he should own the home. I remembered Elvis Jr. mentioning he tried to get into a public housing apartment through MDHA the week before. So, I suggested we call the MDHA contact. They informed me MDHA did have an apartment for Elvis Jr. I told Elvis Jr. I would help him move so we would not have to go before the judge. He agreed.

Moving day came, and I hired some guys to move Elvis' stuff. As the movers loaded up, I took Elvis down to the apartment to get him settled in. He rode in the truck with a cat in a cardboard box to sneak into the apartment complex. I then raced back up to the property and changed the locks. Phew! . . . Elvis has left the building.

The Elvis apartment needed to be gutted, which put the project over budget. My big mistake, though, was that I based the comparables for the home without factoring in how close this home was to a very busy street. It was so close that one could hear from the back porch someone ordering a burger and fries at the nearby drive-thru. Therefore, the home sat on the market because it was overpriced due to the location. I then hired a real estate agent, an expert in the neighborhood, who priced it correctly.

Unfortunately, by the time it sold after the extra renovation costs, loan, and other holding costs, I lost about $20,000. I was also newly married, and I felt like a failure to my wife. However, once the property sold, it freed my energy and mind to work on new deals, and I made back that lost money quickly.

EVALUATING PROPERTY

Once you have a grasp of property values, evaluating a deal is relatively easy. The other missing part of the equation is estimating construction costs. If the property is an existing home needing updates, the experienced real estate agent will either have experience in renovation costs or know a contractor who can give an estimate. For new construction a general contractor can give you a "ballpark" price per square foot to build. The equation is:

$$(ARV \times 70\%) - construction\ costs = Max\ Offer$$

ARV stands for After Repaired Value. That is the retail value you have determined from comparables and consulting with a real estate agent. The reason you multiply by 70% is factoring 10% for holding costs and closing costs to purchase and sell or refinance (if you plan to rent property) plus a 20% net profit.

Consider this scenario. You see a For Sale By Owner sign in a yard, and the asking price is $130,000. There are so many overgrown trees you can barely see the front façade. This is in an area you have been researching, where most homes sale for over $200,000. The owner has already moved out of state and has two mortgages, does not have the funds to renovate the home, and needs to sell.

You make arrangements to view the inside and bring your contractor with you. The interior is in decent shape but needs some cosmetic updates. You both decide that the renovations needed would cost about $30,000. With help from your real estate agent, a conservative resell price after renovations (ARV) is $220,000. Using the "Quick Investment Math" equation, ($220,000 x 70%) - $30,000 = $124,000. Your initial offer is less than $124,000 to leave room for negotiating.

FARMING AN AREA

Farming an area is a great strategy. Most of my active investing career, I narrowed down buying property in one zip code. In the early 2000s, I was afraid of investing in other areas. However, with today's technology, there are now many ways to research and get comfortable investing in other cities and states. Plus, you might live in a market that is expensive or does not fit your investing criteria. There are websites like Zillow that have a lot of information including the ability to run comps. Property tax records are public information and can be found including maps and ownership history of a property and zoning. There are also some subscription-based websites with powerful tools and information such as Propstream , Property Radar, and DealMachine. You can also find a real estate agent in that area to video or live stream a walk-thru of a property.

One of my borrowers for hard-money loans lives in Oregon and invests in East Tennessee. She has a marketing strategy to generate leads and buy great deals; she also has a few contractors she uses with a local real estate agent to help oversee the properties. She then leases the homes and refinances them into a long-term loan.

Similar to the Oregon resident investing in Tennessee, I have sold properties in the Nashville area and reinvested in Clarksville and Chattanooga. I have property managers in both of those cities and spend very little time on those properties.

GENERATING LEADS

As discussed in Chapter 2, networking both in person and online, as well as farming an area, will generate possible leads. It is best to concentrate on a few methods that fit your lifestyle. If you enjoy hunting for deals then driving for dollars, searching online, and direct mail might be a good fit. The DealMachine app is a subscription to not only find deals but automate your marketing. Websites like Roofstock, Fundrise, and Lofty.ai have available investment properties for sale. If you are constrained for time, then wholesalers and real estate agents feeding you leads is ideal. With a little bit of networking, you can find the main wholesalers who are professional and doing a high volume of transactions. Once you find the right real estate agent, they can set up auto notifications of new listings that fit your criteria to be emailed to you.

Casting your net wide by using these methods and just telling friends, family, and co-workers what you are looking for will produce the leads to purchase your first deal. Be patient when finding the property that fits your criteria. If you don't stick to this rule, you might regret it, like the second investment property I purchased. I felt desperate to find a deal and ventured outside of my area of interest in a rural community an hour from my house. After numerous long drives back and forth, it took me two years to sell and I only made a small profit.

HOW SHOULD I ORGANIZE?

Another question first-time investors often ask is "Should I buy in my personal name or set up an entity like an LLC?" This question is asked with asset protection and tax exposure in mind. You should consult your CPA and an attorney who knows the laws of the state where the property is located and the state where you reside. However, if you are just starting to build assets, for your first residential property, it is okay to purchase the property in your personal name, obtain an umbrella insurance policy for added protection, then consult after the purchase with the professionals. Moving a property from your personal name to an entity can be easily done at a small expense.

The book *Rich Dad, Poor Dad* by Robert Kiyosaki was first published in 1997, the year I graduated from college. I am not a big book reader, and I forget who recommended the book to me. However, it instantly caught my attention, so I immersed myself into every page and read it rather fast. I then read his other books or listened to them (on cassette tapes). If you have any interest in starting a business or how to get out of the "rat race," I highly recommend his books.

One of the tips Kiyosaki writes about is that his companies were formed in Delaware. He explained it was easy to do because the laws and taxes were favorable for businesses in that state. Another point he makes is to have a good team of professionals, especially attorneys and accountants. The author states he is happy to pay those professionals for their time because their expertise is valuable. That was the second point I heard but did not follow at first.[6] Why? I did not have the money to pay expensive attorneys and accountants. That decision ended up costing more money, heartache, and time in the long run.

One of the benefits of setting up a Limited Liability Company(LLC) is that, if the corporation gets sued, your personal assets are protected. When I first started real estate investing, I did not have any personal assets besides a Chevy S-10 pickup truck worth about $2500. In 2002, I first set up my LLC based in Delaware like Kiyosaki did, although the purpose of my business was to buy and sell properties in Tennessee. I did not hire an attorney nor consult an accountant.

Tax season came around in 2003, and I was referred to a CPA from another real estate investor. When I told him that I had an LLC formed in Delaware, he said, "You don't want to do that, you will be taxed as a

6   Robert Kiyosaki, *Rich Dad, Poor Dad: What the Rich Teach Their Kids about Money—That the Poor and the Middle Class Do Not!*, 2009, http://ci.nii.ac.jp/ncid/ BA50082780.

foreign entity by the State of Tennessee." Fortunately, I had not made any money in that first year. So, I paid a few hundred dollars to dissolve the LLC in Delaware and formed the LLC in Tennessee; again, I filled out the paperwork myself.

Fast forward to 2008: I had been married since 2005 and was starting to grow my business. My wife's friend was a tax attorney, and I met with him and a colleague of his who happened to be one of most highly regarded tax attorneys in Nashville.

As they looked over my paperwork they asked about my operating agreement. I did not have one.

They asked, "Why are you taxed as a corporation?"

I did not know. I just checked a box that made sense to me when filling out the paperwork with the state back in 2003. As my face turned red and my heart fell into my stomach, the attorneys then went into a long explanation about why that was a costly decision and recommended I dissolve that LLC by year end and start a new one.

As I have learned, attorneys typically recommend talking to a CPA regarding a big change that will affect your taxes, and they should. I then had to pay my CPA for a couple of conference calls and meetings to hash out the details.

To accomplish this involved getting appraisals on the properties held in the current LLC. That cost over $1,000. I then had a tax payment of about $18,000 to move them into the new LLC. This was going to be less expensive than not moving them over time, but it was a painful and costly lesson. As discussed in Chapter 2, books and seminars about real estate investing and business have been immensely helpful in my career. We can read every book written about a topic and still not hear the advice or follow it. Taking advice from professionals who are experts in their field is well worth the rate they charge.

Chapter 5

The Water Is Warm, Step on In!

WHEN YOU GET INTO A hot tub, you don't need to test the water. You already know it is warm. The spa even tells you what the temperature is, so you don't have to guess. Now that you have learned about the different types of investing, the importance of education and networking, and strategy to purchase, the guessing game is over, and it is time to take action. There are two methods to purchase property: the Traditional Method and what I call the Straightforward Method.

THE TRADITIONAL METHOD FOR PURCHASING REAL ESTATE

There are seven easy steps to the traditional method:

1. Narrow Your Focus.

2. Generate Leads.

3. Conduct Due Diligence.

4. Make the Offer.

5. Secure Financing.

6. Close the Transaction.

7. Manage Your Asset.

We have already discussed narrowing down your focus and generating leads, so let's dive into the rest of the Traditional Method.

Due Diligence

Prior to making an offer, or once a property is under contract with certain contingencies in place, do your due diligence. That means taking reasonable steps "in order to satisfy a legal requirement, especially in buying or selling something."[7]

In simple terms, due diligence is conducting research and investigation about the property to mitigate risk. For example, you want to verify the lease terms (by reviewing the lease agreement) if you are looking at a rental property for sale with an existing tenant. Another common example involves purchasing with a home inspection contingency. You as the buyer would hire a professional home inspector to inspect the mechanicals, structure, and cosmetics of the home. If you find something unexpected that would be an additional cost to you as the buyer, you can either back out of the contract, agree to move forward, ask the seller for a price reduction, or ask the seller to make the repair prior to closing.

Other common due diligence items include zoning verifications, codes violations, flood plain location, and utilities. Consulting an experienced real estate agent who has experience is crucial in this process. This is also a time to ask the seller questions so you can cater your offer to their needs and make it a win-win transaction. Ask questions such as Why are you selling? Are there any immediate repairs needed? What do they plan to do with the funds when they sell? If the seller has a mortgage, ask about the terms and balance.

Here is a story all about due diligence. Several years ago, a business partner, Thomas Mattingly, and I made a trip up to Clarksville to look at a

---

7 "Due Diligence Definition & Meaning," Dictionary.Com, December 10, 2020, https://www.dictionary.com/browse/due-diligence.

six-plex and a vacant house that were priced under value (so we thought). We met the agent and owner at the properties. As an investor, you know that you can find a good deal when the owner is a "tired landlord." If you looked up "tired landlord" in a dictionary, you would see this guy's picture. He worked a full-time job in Nashville, a one-hour commute, and was self- managing his rental properties. He walked around slowly with slouched shoulders, dragging his feet like he was pulling a heavy cart up a hill. He hardly had the energy to smile or talk. He bragged that he was the cheapest rent in town; however, three of the six apartments and the house were vacant.

We put together an offer for both properties, dropped it by the agent's office, and headed back to Nashville. On the drive back, they called and countered. We countered back. They accepted. Thomas and I were high fiving in the car.

We went back up to the property about one week later to conduct an inspection. We went inside the house first. It was evident that homeless people had broken in through the window and had been using the bathroom. The water was off so you can imagine the smell. We noticed some blankets and a mattress in the shed and carport. A local "gang" had marked their territory by spray painting the wooden carport wall "Chapel Street Thugs." I guess this was their latest meeting place. At this point, we didn't know if we should laugh or cry.

Finally, we went over to inspect the six-plex. We did discover that one of the units had a mold problem. When we entered another vacant apartment, I noticed a suspicious guy walking from the side of the building out to the street. Thomas went across the street to take a picture of the apartment from the sidewalk.

As Thomas was snapping the photo, a shirtless guy strutting down the street approached him.

"Why you takin' pictures of the crack house?" he asked.

"This is a crack house?" Thomas replied.

"Oh yeah!" replied the shirtless man.

Again, we didn't know if we should laugh or cry.

Thomas and I both grew silent, but we both knew what each other was thinking. As we were getting into our car to drive around the neighborhood, another shirtless neighbor pulled up in his car, parked, got out and stood across the street staring us down. He looked like a lineman for the Tennessee Titans. Then, we noticed the same "suspicious guy" from earlier standing on the street corner a block away.

At that point we did a mental recap and put the pieces together: gang spray paint, house broken into, suspicious guy at the six-plex, six-plex labeled as "The Crack House" by shirtless guy number one, large shirtless guy number two across the street with a cold "you don't belong here" stare, and the same suspicious guy hanging on the street corner looking to make "a sale."

As we drove out of the neighborhood, Thomas and I were still both quiet as it all started to sink in. We saw a police car parking at a convenience store, and we pulled in to get first-hand feedback on the neighborhood. We approached the policeman and asked him about the street the properties were on and he said, "I wouldn't have any property over there. There are a lot of second- and third-time offenders, guys getting out of jail that hang out over there. Unless you want some gray hair like I have, I wouldn't buy property over there." We shook his hand and said, "Thank you for your time." That was the nail in the coffin. We called the listing agent, and we backed out of the deal since we had an inspection contingency. Looking back on it the next day, we just laughed and asked, "Why you takin' pictures of the crack house?"

Making the Offer

This is where first time investors start to get butterflies in their stomach. If you purchased your personal residence, you think back to the long "contract" with a lot of blanks to fill in. Decisions like amount of earnest money, contingencies, inspections, and the date to close, even with the assistance of a real estate agent, can be overwhelming. However, I recommend the KISS (Keep It Super Simple) method for property investments. As the buyer in most cases for residential property, simplifying the process for the seller is typically the best route. In these situations, I use a two-page contract that is easy to understand. The seller might want an attorney to review the contract if the contract is long and has a lot of legal jargon. That extra step costs time and money and might cause the deal to fall through. If you have done all your due diligence, write up an all-cash offer with no contingencies, and let the seller decide when the closing date should be to accommodate their situation. If you are not confident in writing an all-cash offer with no contingencies, add in an inspection contingency for a certain time period to give yourself extra time, but lock up the property before the competition makes other offers.

Financing

It is important to have a plan in place with how to pay for the property before making an offer. That way you can write the offer as a cash purchase with no loan contingency. Funding your first deal is covered later in this chapter.

Closing the Transaction

Closing the transaction is essentially signing the legal papers to consummate the transaction and paying the funds needed for the transaction. The real estate attorney or title company will perform a title search to validate that the title is clear. They will also prepare a settlement statement that explains the financials of the transaction, including all the costs to the buyer and seller.

Administration

You must get organized from a bookkeeping and accounting perspective now that you officially own an investment property. Treat the investment like a business. Scan and save the closing documents for future reference and for your CPA. Set up systems and reminders for tasks and oversight.

THE STRAIGHTFORWARD METHOD

There are a number of ways to easily enter into real estate investing, some people do not think to do. A residential rental property is arguably the best property for a first-timer. If you own a home, one of the easiest methods to own an investment property is converting your personal residence to a rental property. Most Americans sell their personal home and use that equity to purchase a more expensive home. This is called "Moving up in house." However, there are many advantages to not selling. For one, the loan is already in place. If necessary, using the equity from your residence, obtaining a HELOC is how to purchase the next home to move into without selling.

Another advantage is a capital gains exclusion if you qualify. If you live in your personal residence at least two years then lease the property a maximum of three years after you vacate, you could avoid a capital gains tax. Consult a CPA to calculate the tax consequence.

The IRS Website states: If you have a capital gain from the sale of your main home, you may qualify to exclude up to $250,000 of that gain from your income or up to $500,000 of that gain if you file a joint return with your spouse.

Qualifying for the Exclusion

In general, to qualify for the Section 121 exclusion, you must meet both the ownership test and the use test. You're eligible for the exclusion if you have owned and used your home as your main home for a period aggregating at least two years out of the five years prior to its date of sale. You can meet the ownership and use tests during different two-year periods. However, you must meet both tests during the five-year period ending on the date of the sale. Generally, you're not eligible for the exclusion if you excluded the gain from the sale of another home during the two-year period prior to the sale of your home.

Multi-Family Units

Another easy method if you do not own your personal residence is to purchase a duplex or other small multi-family property as your primary residence and live in one unit and earn passive income from the other units. As a personal residence, the loan terms are more favorable. Learning the rental business and property management would be very convenient as well.

If you have cash savings or set up a HELOC to access home equity for a down payment, purchasing a residential rental can also be fairly simple. Your real estate agent can set up email notifications of new listings on the MLS based on your criteria (location, price, property type, etc.). There are numerous websites with investment properties for sale such as Roofstock, Zillow, Lofty.ai, Fundrise, Crowdstreet, and Redfin. Some of these sites are crowdfunding opportunities for as little as $50, like purchasing a stock but with the tax advantages and appreciation. Participation ranges from single family to large commercial projects. Some crowdfunding requires you to be an accredited investor; some do not. To be an accredited investor, a person must have an annual income exceeding $200,000 ($300,000 for joint income) for the last two years with the expectation of earning the same or a higher income in the current year. A person is also considered an accredited investor if they have a net worth exceeding $1 million, either individually or jointly with their spouse. The SEC also considers a person to be an accredited investor if they are a general partner, executive officer, or director for the company that is issuing the unregistered securities.

NON-TRADITIONAL METHODS

Non-traditional methods to enter the real estate investing arena are fair exchanges, joint venture partnerships, and financial participation.

Fair exchanges are trading your time, credit, or expertise in another area with a real estate investor. Julio Bareto, mentioned earlier, specializes in affordable housing in Baltimore, Maryland. He has a mentoring program to teach others how to rehab homes for rent. In exchange, the intern devotes either their time or their credit to obtain the loan for the project. You can also intern for a full-time real estate investor. In exchange for your time assisting in operating the business, the experienced investor provides you with hands-on training. Then, when you are ready, you can form a partnership on your first deal.

If you have credit or funding options, a joint-venture partnership with an active investor is a great way to learn investing. If you have more time than funds and enjoy finding deals, take a deal to an active investor and, instead of making a wholesale fee, ask to partner on the deal to learn the process from start to finish.

They are many ways to participate financially in real estate investing. If you are an accredited investor, there are more options such as syndications. A syndication is pooling capital from a group of others. These are typically used for a multi-family acquisition or other large commercial projects. Depending on the deal, you may or may not need to be an accredited investor. Setting up a self-directed IRA account to invest those funds into a syndication, as well as other methods, is a way to participate not many people are educated about. A self-directed IRA is a retirement account set up by a custodian and allows you to invest in real estate, even originate a loan leveraged by real estate as well as other alternative investments. More information about this topic can be found on irainnovations.com..

Your situation and the area of real estate that interests you will dictate what method or methods you pursue to find that first deal.

FUNDING YOUR FIRST DEAL

You might be asking at this point, How do I pay for this first investment property? There are various forms of financing besides cold hard cash such as the following:

- A traditional mortgage
- An in-house loan from a small community bank
- Hard-money loans
- Private loans
- A financial partner
- A HELOC (Home Equity Line of Credit)
- Seller financing

A mortgage similar to a loan for your personal residence needs to be in your personal name and for residential property only. A mortgage broker has government and company guidelines to abide by. Your credit and income are a factor, and the time of the transaction typically takes longer than the others listed above. Providing financials and other documentation to obtain this type of loan can be time consuming. Appraisals are required and the underwriting process can be strict. There are limits on the number of investment loans in your personal name; however, with a down payment, a long-term rental loan is a good fit for these loans. The rate and term will typically be the most competitive.

An in-house loan at a community bank is a business loan secured by the real estate. Building relationships with bankers originating these loans is a key element for obtaining these loans. Residential and commercial properties can be obtained with these types of loans. Income and credit are also a factor. Appraisals and financials are also required, but the underwriting and approvals can be more efficient than the mortgage process since the process is more relationship-based and the decision makers work closely together. These banks will do construction loans and rental loans. These rental loans are nicknamed "mini-perm" loans. The rate is typically slightly higher than a mortgage with amortization of ten, fifteen, and twenty years. The rate is fixed for a short term like three or five years, hence the name "mini-perm." With a good relationship established, the loan is renewed for another short term with a new fixed rate based on the current market rate.

Hard money loans are easy money because they are based more on the real estate. These are originated by a broker or an individual professionally lending their own funds and others as well. The process is typically fast, especially dealing with the smaller, hard-money lenders. Your credit is a factor, but the lender is basing their decision more on the current or future value after improvements on the property. The interest rates are in the double digits but when factoring in the ease of securing the loan and the speed to close the transaction compared to bank financing, this type of loan is desirable by many investors.

Private lending is like hard-money loans but is financing that you, as an investor, raise from individuals such as family and friends. You and your private lender can negotiate the terms that make it a win-win for both parties.

A financial partner is simply an equity partner into the investment. You are the active investor with the acquisition and management of the property, whereas the financial partner provides the funds. The equity split is negotiated to provide a win-win.

If you have equity in your personal residence, obtaining a HELOC is rather simple. Local and national banks originate them and the costs to obtain are relatively low. The term is typically seven to ten years and are interest only. The benefit is that you are a cash buyer once this product is set up. You can then gain permanent financing later and pay back your HELOC, thus providing you another opportunity to purchase another investment. This method takes discipline to only use the HELOC for investment purposes that create additional income.

Seller financing or owner financing is when the seller agrees to an installment of payments instead of a lump sum at the sale. They essentially become the bank for you as the buyer. There can be tax advantages to the seller, especially if it was an investment property. There are no loan costs for you as the buyer, and the time to close the transaction is relatively fast. The terms are also negotiated like the private lender and financial partner.

Chapter 6

Swimming in the Deep End

I REMEMBER WHEN MY PARENTS finally gave me permission to swim in the deep end as a kid. I proved to them I was a good enough swimmer and thus this gave me more freedom to venture in all areas of the pool with less supervision. At the same time, I couldn't goof off and horseplay in the deep end like I could in the shallow end, where I could stand up. I had to tread to keep my head above the water. Now that you own or have invested in real estate, either through the easy method or traditional method, you must implement systems and strategies to keep afloat. No matter if your investment is considered active or passive, acting as a lifeguard is important.

You need to be able to speak intelligently with your professional team members to effectively run your business. If you are applying for a loan and your banker requests your year-to-date income statement and balance sheet, do you know what those are? How long would it take you to prepare? All these professionals have a certain vernacular, and having basic knowledge will help you better communicate and understand them.

Confer with these professionals to avoid feeling overwhelmed. Sourcing referrals is easier than ever before. In addition to asking friends and family, post a question on local real estate investors group pages on Facebook. If there are multiple responses to the same referral, that is a good sign. Cross reference them with online reviews on their own website, social media, as well as web browser reviews.

Title companies, real estate attorneys, and real estate agents have already been covered in a previous chapter.

PROPERTY MANAGER

If your first property is a residential rental property, the big decision is to hire a property manager or manage the property yourself. There are different philosophies on what route to take. For example, if you own a duplex and live in one unit and lease the other unit, then self-managing can be convenient to show the property and oversee. The tenant might also interact with you, and the lines could blur between friendly neighbor and property manager. That could build a relationship where they stay longer, or they could abuse the maintenance policy and you may feel less inclined to increase rent during renewals. A property manager would provide a buffer, but you would not get the hands-on experience to learn how property managers operate.

Interestingly enough, when I first began buying rentals, I was frequently asked, "Are you the landlord or do you have a property manager?" Back in the early 2000s, all full-time investors I encountered recommended that I self-manage. They had horror stories of bad property managers not being organized, mishandling funds, and leasing to unqualified tenants. They scared me into figuring out property management myself. Having an engineering mindset and managerial experience, I found out that I was pretty good at it, but I didn't like it because it took my time away from looking for other deals.

For maintenance issues, I was the middleman between the contractor and tenant and often met the contractor at the property. For leasing, I took numerous phone calls and set up showings for unqualified prospective tenants and then met them at the property, if they showed up. I then learned to qualify them over the phone and then in the listing for lease, so I only received inquiries from pre-qualified prospects. I set up multiple showings around the same time and asked them to call to confirm the appointment on their way. For rent collection and accounting, I went from using spreadsheets to buying software for rent collection and tracking.

After several years, I hired an office manager who handled the leasing calls and appointments, rent collection, and bookkeeping. I hired a full-time maintenance contractor who would coordinate with the tenants and sub-contractors if needed. I was still very involved with managing the office manager, the maintenance guy, and the bookkeeping.

My office manager decided to leave less than four years after starting. At that time, new local property managers were in business that were professional and they used improved management software that was readily available due to technology advancements. I then transitioned away from hands-on management to hands-off management by hiring a property management company. I managed the property manager, freeing up a lot of time. That decision ended up being one of the best decisions of my career. I was able to concentrate on acquisitions, and my development business grew shortly after.

There is value in self-managing to gain experience. If you purchase your first rental property and want to manage it yourself, go for it. If you want to expand your business effectively, I suggest having a plan in place to advance to the hands-off management stage quicker than I did. You will see the rewards in due time.

When I transitioned my rental portfolio over to a property manager, I learned I was not charging market rent on several properties. Since the property manager managed hundreds of properties, they had a better pulse on the rental market. In addition, they had built a large social media following to attract prospects, therefore filling vacancies rather quickly. Their systems and market knowledge brought value which, in turn, offset the cost I was paying them.

CERTIFIED PUBLIC ACCOUNTANTS

I cannot stress the importance enough of not only hiring a qualified accountant but learning the basics of accounting yourself. I have made a lot of mistakes in my real estate investing career, but a big one was not educating myself early about the basics of accounting and bookkeeping. Instead, I was self-taught over several years, making numerous blunders and pretending to know what my CPA was talking about. In all the courses and seminars I have attended over the last twenty-plus years, I have noticed that learning accounting and bookkeeping is not stressed enough. Honestly, it is hardly mentioned.

In college, friends enrolling into the class Accounting 101 thought it was going to be an easy A and then regretted taking the class or even dropped it before it brought down their GPA. I was majoring in engineering and was always good at math, so I thought it couldn't be that difficult. However, they scared me enough not to take the class. I regret that decision.

Over the past several years, I have had some beginner investors reach out to me for advice. I have sought advice from experienced investors in my career, so I am glad to meet or set up a phone call with them. I cannot stress learning accounting and bookkeeping enough. Accounting and bookkeeping are imperative for any small business owner. Owning even one property is not only an investment but a business. Find an accountant who has other real estate investor clients. Here are some reasons it is so important to hire a CPA.

Fraud

CPAs will keep you out of jail. A slight exaggeration, but the point is they know the law better than you regarding the IRS tax code and will help you avoid tax fraud.

Save Money

CPAs are knowledgeable about tax savings. Tax codes are added and removed depending on politicians, and CPAs keep up to date, as it is their job to do so. They can consult you on tax deductions and credits, thus reducing your tax liability.

Save Time

CPAs will save you time so you can concentrate on your business.

BUSINESS STRUCTURE

CPAs are consultants for corporate structure. If you decide to form a business entity, they can educate you about the state and federal tax consequences for the different entities. It is also recommended to consult an attorney on business structure as well.

BOOKKEEPERS

For several years while I was teaching myself accounting and doing my own bookkeeping, I made numerous mistakes. Mistakes become very time-consuming and frustrating during tax preparation, as just one mistake in bookkeeping can have a domino effect of other problems in the books. I had other tasks to do that made better use of my time. Mistakes are expensive, and I had to pay my CPA for more of his time to fix my mistakes.

I have hired several office managers over the years, and most of them state on their résumé "proficient in QuickBooks." I found that they knew the basics of QuickBooks but did not know real estate bookkeeping. Service-related business bookkeeping is income in + expenses out = net profit. Retail business has inventory in addition to income and expenses. However, in real estate you have multiple property and asset types. Buying and selling property, depreciation, and amortization all need to be entered into the accounting software properly. With one property, you may only need a bookkeeper once or twice a year, but hiring one is well worth it before sending your financials to your CPA.

I cannot stress enough the importance of learning the basics of accounting and bookkeeping if you want to be a real estate investor. Take an online class, read a textbook, or buy "Accounting for Dummies."

REAL ESTATE ATTORNEYS (EVICTIONS AND LAWSUITS)

Some real estate attorneys who handle transactions and closings also handle evictions and lawsuits. However, some do not. One would hope not to need an attorney for evictions and lawsuits, but some tenants run into financial issues and we live in a "sue-happy" society. If you have a property manager, they will handle evictions and have an attorney they frequently use. Leasing issues are not the only potential problems. I have been sued over a fence before. Easements, encroachments, survey mistakes, and improper property convenance are these attorneys' areas of expertise. I recommend getting a couple of referrals for these lawyers and calling them just so you make a connection in advance of needing them. Hopefully, you won't need them.

CONTRACTORS (GENERAL & SUBS)

I have so many stories about contractors that I could write another book just about them. A general contractor (GC) will be valuable when you are figuring out construction costs if you are purchasing a property that needs updates and repairs. Again, getting referrals from real estate agents and other investors is recommended. There are different types of general contractors. You don't want to hire a GC that mainly works with homeowners doing custom renovations. You want a GC that works for developers and other flippers. Subcontractors (subs) for plumbing, electrical, HVAC, and roofing are great to have in your "rolodex" as well.

There are four main traits of a contractor: quality, reliability, honesty, and affordability. I have yet to find a contractor that has all four traits.

If you find three of these qualities in a contractor, build a relationship and treat them well. Bring their crew drinks on a hot day, treat them to lunch, or give them a year-end bonus. Quality and affordability are a rare marriage. In my experience, if a contractor has these two traits, they will either lack reliability or honesty or both. The detriment will cost you time and money. When I was rehabbing multiple homes and managing projects without a GC in the early stages of my career, I put affordability as a top priority when hiring contractors. Over time I learned quality, reliability, and honesty were worth the price.

I was referred to a roofer from a mortgage broker in the mid 2000s and built a good working relationship with them because they were affordable, reliable, and did quality work. The crew was a gaggle of family and friends. They would show up piled in a couple of trucks. They were hard-working good ol' boys. For the sake of this story, let's call them AMC roofing. Let's refer to the owner as Jethro and his son as Junior.

As I began to do more extensive renovations, Jethro offered to perform other jobs such as framing and other miscellaneous work. Since I had built a rapport with them, and they had proved affordable and reliable, I decided to hire them for tasks other than roofing. One home I was renovating to sell on Tennessee Avenue had a lot of junk and debris in the crawl space that needed cleaning out before vapor barrier plastic could be installed. I asked them to take photos of the finished job to prove they had done the work since I did not plan to crawl under the home myself. I remember when they called informing me they were finished and thinking it seemed very fast to finish that job. However, they showed me the photos, and they had a track record of working fast with a large crew of workers. I also went to the home and peeked under the house from the crawl space door. I didn't see any debris in the yard outside the crawl space door, but I didn't question them, and I paid Junior for the job.

I sold that property, and a few months later AMC roofing started to show their true colors. I asked Junior for a bid to build a new deck off a home I was renovating to sell. I also received a bid from another contractor I had used that built decks and fences. I decided to use the other contractor because they were a little less expensive and built a quality deck in the past. Jethro and Junior were upset that I didn't hire them. Junior called me, raising his voice, saying I took away his Christmas money. When I arrived at the property, AMC roofing was working on the roof and the other contractor had started the deck and a confrontation ensued. Jethro then confronted me, yelling just a few inches from my face. I stood there calm and collected, thinking, *They have just fired themselves.* Jethro called me later and apologized, but the damage was done. I did not hire them ever again. Their non-professional actions lost them $20,000-$50,000 of gross revenue per year by losing me as a customer.

Three years later, the homeowner of the Tennessee Avenue home was selling the property and the new buyers hired a home inspector. A routine part of a home inspection is to examine under the home to observe the floor joists and look for any issues with duct work, electrical, plumbing lines, moisture issues, and debris or trash. I received a call from the real estate agent informing me that the home inspector found debris in the back corner of the crawl space under the vapor barrier.

At that point, I then realized that was why AMC roofing finished that job so quickly. Even though it was years later, I ended up doing the right thing and hiring someone to clean out the debris for a second time. That contractor was affordable, reliable, and performed quality work when roofing, but cut corners doing other jobs and was dishonest.

Here's some advice about receiving contractor referrals. From my experience, I have learned that sometimes a contractor will not have the same traits with one client as they will with another. I have been asked for contractor referrals from many friends and family members over the years. Sometimes a friend or family member would report back that they did not have a good experience with a contractor I had recommended. Initially, this puzzled me. Then, I realized that a contractor-client relationship is predicated on expectations. Also, when I used a contractor on multiple projects, I learned their habits, strengths, and weaknesses and adjusted my expectations accordingly. What I began to do when referring contractors was give first a disclaimer telling that, just because I refer a contractor, I am not promising that they will do a great job for them. I then give a brief overview of their strengths and weaknesses in relation to the four traits: quality, reliability, honesty, and affordability.

LICENSED VERSUS NON-LICENSED CONTRACTORS

If affordability is important to you, hiring non-licensed contractors to save money may be tempting but will cost you. Again, I am speaking from experience. Contractors that need a license are general contractors, electricians, plumbers, and mechanical (HVAC) contractors. I was once referred to an electrician who was not licensed, and he installed the wrong wire for a dryer in a rental property. The tenant called after the installation to inform me the outlet was smoking. The incident cost extra time and money and endangered my tenant and my property.

Not only is using licensed contractors important, but even more so is that you or your general contractor is working with the actual licensed contractor applying for the permit and inspections. I have had several sub-contractors tell me they were licensed when in fact they were working under someone else's license. This cost a lot of frustration, time, and money because the actual licensed contractor had no urgency in pulling permits and calling for inspections.

HANDYMEN OR MAINTENANCE SERVICE COMPANIES

If you decide to self-manage a residential rental property, having a handyman or maintenance company in your contacts is imperative. A handyman can be considered a jack of all trades and master of none. They are more affordable for small maintenance issues that do not require a specialty contractor. Beware of a handyman or maintenance company that informs you they perform large projects or tasks unless your referred source informed you that they do that type of work well. When they work on a task that turns out to be a larger repair and they inform you to contact another contractor to address the issue, that is a good sign.

*

Depending on the type of your first investment, you may not need all of these players on your team. As an investor, you can decide how much you want to be involved or delegate to others. For systems and processes, don't reinvent the wheel. What I have done over the years is learn systems from others and modify them to fit my needs. In the beginning, it might feel like you have to tread fast to keep your head above water. With a good team and systems, you will be floating on your back in no time.

Chapter 7

Ride the Waves

I HAVE NEVER TRIED SURFING, but I have ridden waves with a body board. To catch a good wave, you first need to survey the ocean from the beach and decide where the good waves are located. You then need to be patient and wait for the right wave. Lastly, you take action and jump on the body board and have good timing. Once you do all that, the wave takes you to shore with no effort on your part. The ride is fun, and you have a feeling of satisfaction giving you the desire to try it again.

These steps are similar to becoming a real estate investor as explained in this book. Instead of learning the waves and the currents, you learn about the different types of investing. After education and networking, you need to be patient to find the right deal that fits your situation. You act during the transaction of the purchase, obtaining financing, and putting together your team of professionals. Once your systems and processes are in place, you can switch to autopilot, coasting along like riding the wave to the shore. Success will give you the feeling of satisfaction and want to take the ride again.

J.M. Barrie, the Scottish novelist best known for creating Peter Pan, once said, "We are all failures, at least all the best of us."[8] John Maxwell,

8   James M. Barrie, "Courage," The Rectorial Address Delivered by James M. Barrie at St. Andrew's University, OnlineLiterature.com, May 3, 1922, https://www.online-literature.com/barrie/2088/

in his book *Failing Forward—How to Make the Most of Your Mistakes,* said, "To succeed, you have to be open to problems. You must be open to failure. And as you go up the ladder, you gain the right to get more problems."[9]

These quotes are not to discourage, but to encourage. Back when people still read the newspaper, one of my good friends in real estate, Thomas Mattingly, had an ad in the real estate wanted section titled PROBLEM SOLVER. I first laughed when I saw the advertisement, but he was correct. He and I still say it today. Unlike giving your money to a money manager, real estate investing gives you more control, and with control brings problems to solve. When you expect failures and problems, you have a positive mindset. It is not likely that by reading this book everything will work out just as you want. Of course, that is with most things in life. However, the benefits outweigh the potential issues that might arise, and I hope from reading this book and deciding to jump into real estate investing you realize that is the case.

If you have read this and have doubts about yourself taking action, I have some real-life stories from friends of mine who have used these techniques to enter into real estate investing. They range from someone with an hourly wage to a doctor in Hawaii. The benefit to real estate investing is that, no matter your situation, there is an avenue to participate.

When I was working in financial planning, I learned in training that, "It doesn't matter what you make, it is what you do with what you make." When I was young, I used to think doctors, lawyers, professors and the like were all rich because they had high paying jobs, had nice homes and luxury cars. However, a lot of high earners are broke because they spend the same or more than they earn. A low wage earner who lives frugally, has discipline, and spends less than they earn will have savings to invest.

---

9   John Maxwell, *Failing Forward: Turning Mistakes into Stepping Stones for Success,* HarperCollins Leadership, 2000.

THE HIGH-WAGE EMPLOYEE

My good friend Matt is a doctor who lives in Hawaii. If that is all you know about him, you might judge him to be "rich" according to our society. In fact, his decisions over time might have put him in a better financial position than others in the same shoes. We were roommates after college in Nashville for four years. While I was working, he attended medical school at Vanderbilt University. Had Matt decided to apply and receive student loans for medical school, he would have been in six-figure debt when he started his career several years later. Instead, he enrolled into the Navy officer program, which paid the tuition. After medical school, he was able to serve his time in the Navy as an intern in San Diego and a flight surgeon in Florida, Camp LeJeune, North Carolina, and Hawaii. Once he solidified a job as a radiologist, he could work from home and decided to move to Hawaii in 2016. Hawaii is a very expensive real estate market, and the average home sold for around $900,000 that year. Matt's thinking was to purchase a home larger than needed but rent a portion of the home to offset his expenses. He had never been a landlord before. Matt says, "As long as you have the right mindset, it has become a very good financial move." The term used today is "house hacking." Six years later, the house paid for itself. He now lives there essentially free and has amassed great equity. After getting settled as a first-time landlord, he came across a book titled *Why Doctors Don't Get Rich*. This book motivated him to search for another rental property. Matt saved funds along with a family gift for a down payment to purchase a new construction house near his home that could be rented as a multi-family property. His philosophy is to purchase properties in great condition that yield higher rents with lower maintenance. His plan is long-term, so purchasing after the construction process is worth the price. Matt has gotten the real estate itch, looking for another rental but being patient.

THE SEEKER FOR BETTER RETIREMENT OPTIONS

Bryan Myers works in the music business. When he called his company's 401k manager to inquire about how to invest more for retirement, the manager complimented Bryan, as he was the first one who ever asked him that question. He said, "Everyone else in the business spends instead of saves." The manager then recommended real estate as an alternative to the 401k plan of stocks and mutual funds. At the time, Bryan was a little skittish, based on a recently read book downplaying real estate. Bryan then read *Rich Dad, Poor Dad*, and it sparked him to revisit the real estate idea. The 401k manager gave him two good tips; first, do not over leverage yourself and, second, know the area you are investing. Bryan's wife Lana is a longtime friend with my wife, so one night they brought us some sushi and we talked real estate. Along with giving them some tips, I encouraged them to buy a residential rental, as it would be a good entry to "get their feet wet."

Bryan started his market research. Living in the Nashville area, he quickly learned that the prices for rentals were higher than he wanted to pay. He expanded his search to Birmingham, Alabama, since he grew up there. Bryan was already familiar with the neighborhoods and learned he could buy a similar property for about half the price of one in the Nashville vicinity. He found a few condos listed for sale in neighborhoods he knew and set up a weekend to go visit family and view properties with a real estate agent. He spoke to a mortgage broker, put 20% as a down payment, and, before he knew it, he and Lana were proud owners of their first investment property. After scraping that 1980s popcorn ceiling and a fresh coat of paint, the house was rent ready. He decided to self-manage. Since Bryan's mom and brother live nearby, he calls on them to refer a contractor when needed. Even though the property was purchased for fair market value, less than five years later the property has increased over 60%, they have paid down the mortgage, and increased the rent over time for great cash flow.

CASH FLOW FOR BETTER INCOME

My childhood friend Lee Williams moved away in middle school due to his dad's job. He saw the long hours his dad worked all those years with not much to show for it, and he did not want to replicate. While I was in college, Lee moved back to our hometown of Asheville, North Carolina. He worked at a popular coffee shop with ideas of going to school, and, like most of us in our early twenties, he wasn't real sure what type of work he wanted to do long-term. He also did not want to go into debt with student loans. A few years passed by, and he worked various service jobs and then became the head bartender at a local restaurant and pub.

Lee became disciplined and frugal as a young adult and built good credit. He attended a first-time homebuyer's class through the local affordable housing coalition. At the completion of the class, he received a $6,000 grant to buy a home, with the stipulation he could not sell the home in the first two years. Programs like this are offered in numerous communities nationwide. With $2,000 of his own money along with the grant, he purchased his first home near downtown Asheville. Being single, he had a roommate to offset his expenses (another house hack). After living in that home about ten years, he had a $9,000 down payment for a newly built condo to move into. Lee built great credit with his bank, who held his first mortgage, so they willingly loaned the funds for his second home. For less than $1,000 per year over those ten years of ownership, he was able to keep his first home as a rental instead of selling it. Lee now had cash flow from his first home increasing his income.

About eight years later, Lee had a choice to make on his first home. Either do a major renovation on the home to sell it for top dollar or sell it "As Is." He chose "as is" due to the equity he had built up and the appreciation. Shortly thereafter, he heard about a home that was priced below market and in great condition. He purchased that home with funds from the sale, moved into it, and then rented out the condo. Lee now has a job he enjoys at the hospital three days a week, equity and income from his rental, and a very low monthly payment with great equity in his personal residence.

THE PILOT BECOMES THE DEALER

Several years ago, at a REIN meeting, I posted to the group that I was looking for an intern. I ended up speaking with a younger new investor named Tim, who was eager to learn. He worked at night piloting a cargo plane transporting bank receipts. Finding out that was even a job in the mid-2000s blew my mind. I'm guessing that job is obsolete with the development of technological advances. His job gave him free time during the day to learn real estate investing. Two to three times a week, Tim would come to my home office. I first taught him the basics of wholesaling and direct marketing, then he transitioned to work independently and had me as a springboard to answer questions along the way. After several weeks of dedication, he received a good lead on a property to wholesale. I helped him find a buyer, and we split the wholesale fee. Shortly after, he moved out of town and took his knowledge with him to find his first "flip."

LEARN AND MAKE A RETURN

I mentioned in Chapter 4 about Julio Bareto's program, BREADCORP, in Baltimore, Maryland. BREADCORP, in conjunction with a developer, Ewin Corp One, has multiple purposes that intertwine Julio's two passions of education and improving the lower income community. BREADCORP helps educate first-time homeowners about the buying process and assists them with local grants for financing. Julio's model is to help the city of Baltimore gentrify blocks of neighborhoods where homes have been boarded up vacant for over a decade.

Julio has found that the lower income community has a lot of fear of home ownership simply because the homebuying process is complicated. Most of his homebuyers approach BREADCORP inquiring about renting a home. For ones that want to learn and have just a little bit of discipline, they can change their family for generations. He told me about a sixty-six-year-old veteran who wept when he purchased his home through the BREADCORP program. He was the first of his family to ever own a home. Other family members have followed his footsteps and became homeowners as well.

They also have a program for investors who don't have time to be an active investor but can invest into a fix and flip, net a 20% return, and learn the real estate business through observing the project, monthly updates, and mentoring. The investor then has the option to "cash out" or roll their funds into another project. Another program of BREADCORP gives the investor the option to purchase the home after the renovation to then keep as a rental property.

This is a great program if you are interested in flipping homes to learn the process while partnering with an expert who has the heart to teach while also helping people become homeowners and improving the lifestyle of a community.

WHAT KIND OF INVESTOR ARE YOU?

Everyone's situation and interests are different. As stated before, real estate investing can be overwhelming. Everyone's situation and interests are different. Where should you dip your toe into real estate investing for the first time? The answer depends upon what kind of real estate investor you are. I have identified eight types of investors:

- **The Landlord** invests in residential rental properly for long-term appreciation and cash flow. That role comes with responsibilities such as honing in on a desirable location, acquiring financing, and self-managing or hiring a property manger. It can provide a substantial increase to your net worth over time.

- **The Learner** has more time than financial resources. Learners have the lowest risk tolerance and can benefit from hands-on experience with an experienced, full-time investor. This could lead to possible partnerships with their mentor's connections once they have experience under their belt.

- **The Chunker** enjoys the potential to reap larger profits in a short time. Chunkers make old houses new again, aka "flipping homes." They might also venture into building spec homes or developing land. Construction and design are major components for success, so experience in either or both of these fields is an asset. A higher risk, higher reward mentality is needed.

- **The Dealer** is a mover and shaker. Dealers delight on hunting for good deals, communication with all sorts of people, and connecting with other investors. Sales and negotiating skills are a plus that can be learned by those who wish to become dealers who "wholesale" properties.

- **The Facilitator** is keen on sending out their dollars to return with friends. In other words, they are looking for a return on their investment, also known as passive income. Whether accredited or non-accredited, facilitators invest their funds in small or large amounts through avenues such as crowdfunding or in limited partnerships with other financial partners. Although the returns can be lower than those received by an active investor, facilitators don't need to invest much time. With a few connections and trusted partners, no experience is required.

- **The Partner,** similar to the facilitator, is more hands-off. However, a partner joins forces with one active full-time investor who will fund their endeavours. The equity split between the parties, type of properties, price ranges, and strategies are negotiated before acquiring properties. Financial resources are a must. This partnership allows the active investor to perform what they excel in without concern for funding. Trust and accountability are key to success.

- **The Banker** lends funds to multiple investors as a debt instrument. Instead of being an equity partner with only one investor, the banker has their own funds, either cash or from a line of credit, or raises funds from others. He can also broker loans and make commissions. Hard-money, bridge loans, and even long-term loans help this investor earn high short-term interest or longer term cash flow. Bankers are usually number crunchers who work from an office and discuss deals with active investors. A background in finance or any experience with mortgages is a plus but not necessary.

• **The Claimer** is a long-term buy and hold investor. Claimers do not wish to deal with maintenance or tenants of homes or buildings which demand much of their time to generate income. However, some claimers might seek resource-based land so they can harvest timber or participate in sharecropping to help offset the property cost. This type of investor is usually interested in rural areas but also likes to seek other profitable acquisitions like the dealer.

To help determine the type of investor *you* are, take the quiz at **www.reinvesting.formaloo.co/to9vmi** or scan this QR Code.

Once you determine the kind of real estate investing that feels right for you, you're ready to dip you toe in the water. Get your feet wet. Take what you can from my experience, build wealth, and have fun doing it!

Afterword

WRITING ASSIGNMENTS IN PRIMARY SCHOOLING was tough for me. When it came to creative writing, my mind went blank. One year, we had a standardized test and we were to write about a building we had visited. Nothing came to mind, and I ended up writing about the Empire State Building, which I had never seen in person. News flash: I didn't score well. In junior high, my friends once pointed out, while laughing at me, how I wrote with no left indentation. I would start a new line at a different place every time. I didn't even realize I was doing this. I dreaded reading and writing assignments all through high school and often faked my way through them and somehow still received good enough grades.

I hated reading as a kid. I was slow at reading, and my mind would wander. I could read a page and then not know what I had just read. I would doze off every time I read more than ten pages. Cliff Notes were my best friend in school. If my English teacher gave us quizzes on a reading assignment, I would guess using deductive reasoning and logic and sometimes get the answers correct. Although getting a "B" in eighth grade English, I requested to drop down one level for ninth grade because I would not be required to read over the summer. That was the reason I had Mrs. Sessions, which ended up being a great blessing.

The only books I enjoyed at a young age were the Choose Your Own Adventure books. Why? It gave me control of the story. Very few books I was assigned to read were interesting to me. I always judged the book by its thickness. I would open it up and immediately find out how many pages it contained. I knew if I judged the book too long, I would never finish within the allotted time. Three books I was forced to read in school that interested me were *Lord of the Flies*, *Cather in the Rye*, and *The Great Gatsby*. Now I can understand the common themes of boys or young men on an adventure and exploring new events in life. In my young adult life, I discovered nonfiction books. These were real stories of people and subjects that could improve my situation relating to spiritual, self-help and motivation, leadership, as well as finance and business.

Writing and reading were a struggle, but Math came easy to me. My mom used to call me a "walking calculator". In ninth grade my algebra teacher told me I should be an engineer. At the time I didn't put much stock into her recommendation. My junior year in high school as I started thinking about college, the engineering subject resurfaced. I went to visit a local engineering firm and the two engineers that showed me around told me I should have good writing skills because engineers write a lot of reports. I dismissed that comment. I didn't want to believe that was true. Engineering was math and science combined. Engineers were to solve problems, not write reports. It didn't prevent me from applying to schools with engineering. To this day I do not know how I got accepted into Vanderbilt's school of engineering. After narrowing down my options I chose Vanderbilt even though I was concerned about the high tuition and the strain on my parents and student loans. I put in the effort and graduated with a degree in Civil Engineering.

After college, I worked at an engineering firm and my main job as a project manager was . . . writing reports! I shook my head with a fist in the air in frustration and said, "Those engineers were right!" The type of reports we wrote were mostly boiler plate using templates, and I would literally fall asleep writing them. From the technical writing in college and the many reports written at the engineering firm, this gave me the foundation of my writing style today (except for the boring part hopefully).

When I was growing my development business, West Nashville Living, it was recommended to me to write a blog on a regular basis. Initially, my mind raced back to the days in school when I had writer's block. I begrudgingly agreed to do this to help the brand. Of course I procrastinated, but once I brainstormed on some content and sat down to write, the typing flowed like a creek after a hard rain. I started to get some good feedback from others like "I read your blog. That was really interesting."

When I started Bridge South Investments in 2019, I was again told by the marketing experts to write blogs. I knew I needed to but didn't want to. The same process developed as before with even better feedback. I had family and friends that didn't have an interest in the business reading about real estate and lending emailing me saying, "Great blog!" It was then that I thought maybe I could actually teach through my writing.

In November of 2021, I was invited to attend a week-long course that not only gave me the vision to begin to invest outside of real estate but the practical steps to write a book. One of the first actions I took after that week was writing an outline of this book. During that week, I met Bobby Dunaway, who runs Indigo River Publishing, so, after I drafted my outline, I contacted him to get some advice on the next steps. During our phone call, he said, "Send me the outline; we might be interested in working with you." I was suddenly taken aback. Really, me? Some engineering major who faked his way through English classes? I signed with Indigo River, and the same process of writing blogs began. I would procrastinate and find other work to do instead of writing, but once I carved out time in a quiet place, the words rolled onto the page. I wanted to write the first draft in three months. It took one year.

Once I began the writing process, a business mentor told me that, when the book is released, people are going to contact me seeking further advice. I honestly had not thought that far. With the first draft complete, I began the prep work for my new launch, www.InnovestLife.com.

This book is an avenue into this website to learn more, provide further resources, and assist you to be a successful investor. After taking the quiz and determining what investor type you are, visit www.InnovestLife. com to find further education and ways to invest that fit your situation. I believe everyone should be an investor at some capacity and when the timing is right. If you are saving, you are losing money. We are not in a world of solely investing mutual funds into a 401k or IRA anymore. We must assume Social Security will not be reliable either. We all need to adapt to the current economy and technology to avoid a fixed income in our "senior" years. You have started your journey for success by reading this book. Now continue to not survive but thrive and build generational wealth for your family by taking the next step.

SCAN TO VISIT INNOVESTLIFE.COM

Acknowledgements

WHILE I AM INDEBTED TO numerous friends, family, and colleagues, I am particularly grateful to my parents for giving me the freedom to explore at a young age and to raise me in Asheville, North Carolina. For my sister who has always supported all my endeavours. For Zach Young, for exposing me to real estate investing. For Steve Fouche, my first mentor in real estate. For the Wednesday lunch crew over the years where we shared experiences, laughed a lot, and complained about codes. For my loving, supportive wife Dawn, who has always given me the trust and belief in my career. For the people at Indigo Publishing for believing I had a book and a story to share with others.

Recommended Reading

Rich Dad, Poor Dad by Robert Kiyosaki

Rich Dad's Cash Flow Quadrant by Robert Kiyosaki

Rich Dad's Guide to Investing by Robert Kiyosaki

Think and Grow Rich by Napolean Hill

The Education of Millionaires by Michael Ellsberg

The 7 Habits of Highly Effective People by Stephen R. Covey

Financial Peace by Dave Ramsey

Good to Great by Jim Collins

The Millionaire Next Door by Thomas J. Stanley

Failing Forward by John C. Maxwell

How Real Estate Developers Think by Peter Hendee Brown

Never Split the Difference by Michael Kramer

The Tipping Point by Malcolm Gladwell

Blink by Malcolm Gladwell

Outliers by Malcolm Gladwell

The Upstarts by Brad Stone

What It Takes by Stephen Schwarzman

The Boys in the Boat by Daniel James Brown

Unbroken by Laura Hillenbrand

When Helping Hurts: How to Alleviate Poverty without Hurting the Poor . . . and Yourself by Brain Fikkert

Bibliography

"Benjamin Franklin." *Wikipedia.* August 19, 2023. https://en.wikipedia.org/wiki/Benjamin_Franklin.

"Build Something Real." *Crowdstreet.* 2023. https://www.crowdstreet.com/.

"Build Wealth with Real Estate, One Brick at a Time." *Lofty.* 2023. https://www.lofty.ai/.

Cauble Group. "The Cauble Group Commercial." Cauble Group. 2021. https://www.tylercauble.com/blog/industrial-real-estate.

CoStar Group. "Find Land for Sale." *LandWatch.* 2023. https://www.landwatch.com/.

"Due Diligence." *Dictionary.com.* 2023. https://www.dictionary.com/browse/due%20diligence.

"Do You Know The Meaning of the Phrase 'Time Is Money'?" Avanse Financial Services. 2021. https://www.avanse.com/blog/do-you-know-the-meaning-of-the-phrase-time-is-money#:~:text=The%20origin%20of%20the%20phrase,Remember%20that%20time%20is%20money.%E2%80%9D

"Explore New Opportunities." *IRA Innovations*. 2023. https://irainno-vations.com/.

"Find a REIA." *National Real Estate Investors Association*. 2023. https://nationalreia.org/find-a-reia/.

Hayes, Adam. "Accredited Investor Defined: Understand the Requirements." *Investopedia*. July 4, 2023. https://www.investopedia.com/terms/a/accreditedinvestor.asp.

Hayes, Mark. "'Do You Have Your Real Estate License?'" *Bridge South Investments*. February 23, 2021. https://www.bridgesouthinvestments.com/blog/do-you-have-your-realestate-license.

Hayes, Mark. "Real Estate Investing, Angel Investing, and Private Lending." Bridge South Investments. 2023. https://www.bridgesouth-investments.com/.

"High Yield Returns. Generate Recurring Income." *Percent*. 2023. https://percent.com/.

"Invest in a Real Asset." *FarmTogether*. 2023. https://farmtogether.com.

"Join a Community of Serious Real Estate Investors." *7 Figure Flipping*. 2020. https://www.7figureflipping.com/.

"Live Life on Your Terms with Real Estate Investing." *BiggerPockets*. 2004. https://www.biggerpockets.com/.

"Real Estate Analysis." *Zilcalculator*. 2010. https://www.zilculator.com/.

"Rise above Volatility." *Yieldstreet*. 2023. https://www.yieldstreet.com/.

The Tennessean. "Hal E. Wilson." *Legacy.com*. April 17, 2010. https://www.legacy.com/us/obituaries/tennessean/name/hal-wilson-obituary?id=23435408.

"Your Roadmap to Financial Freedom." *7 Figure Multifamily*. 2020. https://www.7figuremultifamily.com/.

"Zilculator: Real Estate Analysis." *Zilculator*. 2010. https://www.zilculator.com/.

Printed in the USA
CPSIA information can be obtained
at www.ICGtesting.com
LVHW020005090524
779633LV00017B/369